FATHER FIGURE

DWAYNE "COOLI HI" JONES

Published by:
Fortune Publishing Group
E-mail: info@fortunepublishinggroup.com
www.FortunePublishingGroup.com
Phone: (888) 910-6370

ISBN 13 : 978-1-955358-34-7
Printed in the United States of America
Book Cover designed by Skarr Akbar & Max Fortune

Table of Contents

CHAPTER 1
Dear Momma

Dear mother of sons. I hope this reading finds you when you are well, spiritually, emotionally, and mentally. A lot of what I will say will be harsh and direct but please know my intentions are not to hurt. My goal is simple and that is to offer positive insight that will enhance the relationship between mothers and sons and provide a "cheat sheet" for boys and young men to navigate effectively through this thing we call life. With that being said, let's get to it.

Mom, your son is NOT yours. I repeat, your son is not your son. That may sound like an oxymoron but here's why I say this. At birth, the normal female ovary contains about 1- 2 million eggs and that number declines each month. Females are not capable of making new eggs and by the time a girl enters puberty, only about 25% of her lifetime total egg pool remains, around 300,000.

During a female's menstrual cycle, she loses about 1,000 immature eggs (every month) while ovulating only one. Then dad comes along with his sperm and the process begins.

The reason for the brief biology lesson is to point out that so many things must go right and line up in order to conceive a child. None of which you nor the father of your child have any control over. Outside of the new innovative ways to conceive, the most we can do is have sex at a particular time and hope all the dots connect-which means we have no control or say in this process at all. We are depending on our bodies to work as the doctors have said it should. Since we cannot control the outcome (we can only trust and hope things will line up), a phenomenon is needed in which I would call a miracle and miracles come from GOD. So, in essence Mom, your son is not yours, he belongs and comes from GOD.

Again, so many internal biological things must line up perfectly to conceive a child and even with the new innovative ways to conceive, a soul and spirit still needs to be instilled in the embryo and that comes from GOD. Children are gifts from GOD and before you were even born Mom, GOD had plans of gifting you a son. His body and flesh came from you, but his soul and spirit came from the heavens above which was ordered by GOD. You have been chosen by GOD to love, nurture and instill pertinent values into the foundation of his being to fulfill GOD's purpose for his life.

Your Baby Boy

In the early stages of your son's life, there are some important things you must know. You cannot stop things from happening to him nor can you protect him. You don't have that kind of power. Only GOD does. That's why you must have a relationship with GOD so you can pray and ask GOD for things you have no control of. For example, let's say you and your son are at the grocery store and some wacko decides to start shooting. Unless you have a "S" (Superwoman) on your chest, in which we know you don't, you have no way of stopping a bullet from hitting you or your son. You are just as defenseless as your child therefore YOU cannot protect him. Again, no control of what's happening. The more we realize that we don't control anything, the more appreciative we are for GOD's grace and mercy. This is what prayer is for. GOD protects your son. Not you. You can't stop sickness, diseases, or any type of harm to your son. You can only take preventative measures. Only GOD can do things beyond our reach so it's a must that you as Mom stay connected to HIM and pray for your son consistently.

The job that you've been blessed and chosen for has an 18-to-21-year timeline. I'm not against mothers pursuing careers and dreams but please know there's a thin line between goal pursuing and being an effective mom. Normally, one of the two will get slighted. Also, goal pursuing and dream chasing are not to be confused with doing what it takes to provide. In life, you can't have it all. Major sacrifices are required that usually disrupt your life plans to the core. You are now responsible for a human life that was gifted to you by GOD that came from HIM but through YOU! The responsibility is yours (and Dad's) only, not YOUR parents. Grandparents have the OPTION of helping but are not required. Their responsibility was YOU- not the grandchild.

"Me time" is understandable. I hear a lot of moms use this term but keep in mind what the priority is and that is to nurture what GOD has brought into this world, through you (for HIS glory) which is your son. So, in a nutshell, to be the mom your son needs, you must put all your wants and desires on hold, fulfill your GOD given duty as being a mom and then possibly revisit dreams and aspirations later in life. THE ULTIMATE SACRIFICE. Now I know this will not sit well with the modern-day mom and that's okay but just know one day your son will be an adult and will look back at his childhood and I believe he will understand better if mom wasn't around as much because she was working in order to provide for the family rather than mom was out chasing a dream or trying to advance her career. Dream chasers tell themselves "I'm doing this for my family" but in reality, they're doing it for themselves. The child doesn't need the money, success or the "better life". The child needs the presence of a loving mom.

Discipline

In the early stages of your son's life, it's very important to establish a foundation based on love and discipline. If this is done correctly, you won't have as many problems when he's older. Love him but do not spoil him. The bible says, "He who spares the rod hates his son, but he who loves him is diligent to discipline him." Proverbs 13:24.

During the first few years of your son's young life, it is important to instill disciplinary actions (spankings) when the moment calls. This is a very sensitive topic but necessary. It is important to know when to spank your young son and when not to. Spanking should only occur when your young son is able to understand the reason for the spanking. If the young child isn't able to comprehend the "why" behind the spanking, the discipline is pointless. For example, if your toddler walks over to an electrical outlet and touches it out of curiosity, your first response should be a stern verbal correction, to make sure he UNDERSTANDS that mommy is serious. DO NOT TOUCH. But when it's clear to you that he understands and decides to touch it anyway, discipline is needed.

The amount of discipline can vary. For some a simple smack on the hand will do. For others, maybe a pop on the butt. You don't have to overdo it. Remember, the purpose of the spanking is to TEACH the young boy- if you do THIS, THIS will happen. There are consequences for every action. So, if you don't want these consequences, do not take part of this action. You're correcting them, not trying to physically harm them. Also, babies are off limits because babies do not have the capability of comprehending the why- so it would be pointless. Afterwards, you should explain the "why" to your toddler son with a loving tone so he will know that Mom isn't trying to hurt him- she's teaching him.

**Although I understand the reasoning for the "TIME OUT" method I don't completely agree. You're in the process of changing boys into men. It's a cold and cruel world out here and there's no "TIME OUT" for men when they choose to partake in the wrong actions- only harsh punishment. But I get it, some of you parents aren't playing with a full deck and in order to prevent child abuse (which I would NEVER condone), the TIME OUT method is recommended.

Mom, it is important to know that your son doesn't need for you to be tough or stern (only in disciplinary situations). That's Dad or a man's job. Mom, your son needs nurturing and love from you so when disciplining him, lead with love- not an iron fist because in the future as your son becomes older, your iron fist (spankings) will not faze him at all.

When hearing the stories from Generation X and how they were disciplined by their single mothers, often you would hear about the mom's using belts, brooms, shoes, anything they could get their hands on, even extension cords for discipline (beatings- are what they were called back then). But if you noticed, this form of discipline only came from moms- not the dads. The reason being is because as the boy got older, he got bigger and stronger and before mom knew it, her physical spanking didn't affect the son at all. When boys reach a certain age or level of maturity, moms spankings are completely ignored however on the contrast, dads are overexaggerated. A mom can hit her son as hard as she possible can and the boy would just stand there and look at her like she's crazy but if dad or a man plucks the boy, he would drop to the floor from pain. The reason behind this is dads hit came from a different place than moms. In the boy's mind, mom can't hurt me because of the love she has for him (and also because she's a woman) however dads (or a man's) hit is coming from a different place possibly- with the intention to hurt.

That's why mom had to use brooms, shoes, whatever she could get her hands on because her hands and physical strength alone had no effect. Often the son would just stand there and allow the mom to hit on him (no tears) and when the mom resulted to grabbing objects, the son would just attempt to block the hits. In some cases when the son was fed up, he would physically take the object out of mom's hands. The point I'm making is there will come a time when your iron fist becomes ineffective, and spankings will not work. Your son will be bigger and stronger (physically) than you. So, then what will you do? This is why you must lead with love and not an iron fist.

The last thing in this world that any son wants to do is see his mothers feeling hurt. Especially if he's the cause of the hurt. So, at some point you must convert your physical way of discipline to an emotional discipline. When your son does something that requires discipline, let him know that his actions are hurting you. If his actions are severe enough, cry.

Note: Please be mindful with your cries. Mom's if you can, try not to cry around your son too often. When needed, go off to your special hiding place, let your cry out and return when you're done. You don't want your son to see you crying a lot. If so, your tears will lose their value and if you cry while emotionally disciplining him, your tears will not hold any weight.

When a son knows his actions are hurting his mom, he will immediately try to fix things by doing right.

Again, no boy wants to hurt his mother's feels. You are his first and most important relationship on planet earth. To him, you are what love is and seeing you upset (especially because of something he did) is devastating. When to convert physical discipline to emotional discipline is tricky. It's case by case- depending on the child. I would recommend the moment you physically spank your son, and he looks at you like you're crazy and doesn't cry, it's time for change.

PUBERITY

The first ten years of your son's life are the most important. This is when the foundation of his very being is built. It's a must that you teach your son about God and encourage him to have a relationship with the living God. Proverbs 22:6 says, "Train up a child in the way he should go and when he is old, he will not depart from it." God is the ultimate resource and we as seasoned adults know (well should know) that as life goes on, there will come a time when we all will come across challenging situations that God and ONLY God will be able to get us through.

Life has no exemptions. The longer we live, the more highs and lows we will experience. When you instill having a relationship with God in your son, you're providing him with the ultimate resource. Rest assure, there will come a day when he's faced with a challenging issue (or issues) that neither you, Dad, Granny or anyone else can step in and save him from. By knowing God and having a personal relationship with HIM, your son will know where to turn when these situations occur. When life storms arise, he must know where to turn for shelter.

It's also important to teach your son the value of teamwork. If he takes a liking to sports, I strongly recommend signing him up for a youth team of whatever sport he's in to. For those that are not into sports, I would recommend exploring your son interest to see what he likes and signing him up (musical bands, chess/ book clubs, debating teams etc.).

Being a part of a team has many advantages such as, it gives your son an outlet to burn off energy, it allows him to meet others that share's his same interest and also extracurricular activities are known to keep young boys out of trouble because as the old saying goes "An idle mind is the devil's playground". What I just mentioned are all good qualities that teams have but there are so many other pluses that come along with being on a team that are seldom mentioned.

One of my favorites is unfairness/ favoritism. There are so many challenging scenarios that your son could possibly be involved in when he first joins a team. One- he could be the "new guy" on a team where all of the other kids already know each other. Two- he could be joining a team where the coach is the father of the star player that plays the same position as your son. Three- the coach/ instructor could be close friends with the kids on the team parents and shows special interest in those particular kids. All of these scenarios could possibly cause your son to deal with unfairness/ favoritism at a very young age- which is a good thing because we as adults know, unfairness/ favoritism resides in the corporate work field as well. Supervisors giving promotions to employee's that they're sleeping with (or trying to sleep with) or family members and the most infamous one of them all- the click. The ones that hang out together outside of work. Its all the same.

Life is not fair. The best player doesn't always get to play. Just like the most qualified, doesn't always get the job or promotion. If presented, being a part of the youth team could give your son firsthand experience on how to deal with adversities like unfairness/ favoritism at a young age which will help him navigate more effectively if he must face this in the future. It won't be such a shock. He'll be learning how to cope and overcome unfairness without even knowing it. He will recognize (because it will be a familiar look) when these issues are possibly brewing and be able to deal with them accordingly.

Another one of my favorites is learning how to work with others. This is a very important life skill that all human beings should have. When you're a part of a team, you and your teammates are designated specific responsibilities and are held accountable for those responsibilities for the greater good of the team's success therefore you must be able to work well with others. You do your part. I do my part. We help each other when needed and collectively we WIN as a TEAM. Working with others remove's any selfish characteristics that may hide deep within, and it teaches your son that in order to achieve the team goals, partnering with others is necessary. It also teaches your son that in some situations you must depend on and trust others. You cannot do it all by yourself.

Take for an example a professional boxer. To the naked eye, some might think that when the boxer is in the ring fighting, he's in there by himself (a part of this is true) however, what we must realize is BEFORE that boxer stepped into that ring, he was being trained, mentored, and coached by a TEAM for years to prepare him for that fight! Even between rounds, when the boxer goes into his corner, he has a TEAM that's coaching him, treating his wounds, giving him water, etc. The same goes for any individual sport- tennis, golf, swimming and also entertainment- actors, singers, rappers, influencers, TV personalities- there is ALWAYS a team behind the talent so in order to be successful, working well with others is an essential tool that your son must have.

** This life skill transcends into so many adult scenario's- especially in the work field but more importantly, in family. In the household, I have my responsibilities. The other family members have theirs. We help each other when needed and COLLECTIVELY we win as a family by having a healthy home.

My final favorite ingredient of being a part of a team is it pushes your son to work hard for wanted results. 2 Thessalonians 3:10 says "For even when we were with you, we gave you this rule- The one who is unwilling to work shall not eat." As young boys in training to one day become men, it is important to know that this world will give and absolutely owes him nothing! Girls are "given" things for obvious reasons, but boys are given nothing. Everything he wants he must go out and get it and chances are, if he wants it, someone else wants it also. That's why boys- soon to be men must know how to work hard and compete. Put in the work. Make the sacrifices and go after his heart's desires. When on a team, your son must first compete within the team and then compete with opposing teams. Facing off with competition will prepare him for when he's an adult going after an achievement. He will subconsciously know what's required to achieve his goal- HARD WORK and OUTWORKING the competition.

**Losing is also a vital life lesson that being a part of a team teaches. Losing teaches you son that in life you can't win them all but more importantly, it teaches your son how to deal with the feeling of losing and how to bounce back.

TEENAGER

Mom, your son is not your boyfriend. God did not put him in your life to fill the void of your father, husband nor boyfriend. Your son is not your God either so don't praise or worship him, meaning do not put your son before God. Remember, God is a jealous God and I'll stop there- Exodus 34:14. Sometimes, due to the lack of a man's presence, neglect, or the biggest of them all- heartbreak, mom's will often cling to their son with the notion of "this is the one male on earth that will never hurt me because he comes from me and he's literally mine- no one can take him away."

Loving your son this way will damage any meaningful relationship he will have in the future. Keep in mind that you're his introduction to woman and love. You are his very first love. All other loves come after his love experience with you. So, if you're subconsciously loving/ treating him as a spouse (with the kisses, excessive hugging, pampering etc.) you will set the love bar so high, that when he's older, no other woman will be able to reach and that will make him think the woman doesn't love him because it's not meeting the standard of Mom's love which is impossible because no love can compare to Mom's love (except for God). Therefore, no other woman's love will suffice because Mom's overbearing love is now the standard. When he's an adult and in a relationship, the moment he doesn't feel "Mom's love" he will dismiss the woman and run back to your arms because no love trumps the love of Mom. No woman will ever be good enough.

On the flipside of this coin, once your son starts dating, he going to venture off (sexually) because although no love trumps Moms love, the one category Mom cannot cover is sex. We as adults know how powerful sex and intimacy is so when that comes into play, your son will become distant and if you're treating him like a spouse/ boyfriend, the change in behavior will hurt your feelings. It's very possible that you will become jealous and attempt to interfere in your son's relationship to get him to come back to you. Mom, if you can recall, you have probably dated men like this, that have overbearing Mom's that was always sticking her nose in you and your man's business causing problems. You didn't like that mom so don't be that mom to your son's future girlfriend.

Mom, be mindful of how many men you have around your son. Respect is earned, never given. Boys don't like to see any man (except for Dad- and that's only if he's customed to seeing Dad with Mom. In some cases, not even Dad) with their mother so to see multiple men is hard. I'm not suggesting that you shouldn't date and see men but keep your interactions as private as possible. Your son should not meet or be aware of every man you date. The man should earn the right to meet your son. It should be a privilege or a special occasion. That way when you do bring a guy to meet your son, although he may not like it, he will hold the meeting in high regards because its rare. If your son is meeting a new man every few months, the interaction will hold no value and your son could subconsciously start to judge you and think you're promiscuous. Once these thoughts start swimming around in his head, the disrespect and attitude follows afterwards, and you will have no idea where its coming from.

** Always keep in mind that you are his introduction to love and womanhood/ what a woman should be. He hears what you say but more importantly he's watching what you do! Your behavior is the key. The best way to gage your behavior is to ask yourself this question:

Would you want your son to marry someone that's exactly like you (or what you have presented to him)? When you answer this question, be honest and don't take the easy route by saying "I want him to marry someone that's better than me." The question pertains to YOU! Would you be okay with him marrying a duplicate of you? If the answer is no, then you have some work to do.

Father Figure

Mom do not be naked around your son! A son shouldn't see his mom naked or barely dressed on a normal basis. I get it Moms- when you're home, you want to relax and normally that requires coming out of your clothes but keep in mind you have a son- a human being that's wired by physical and visual stimulations so the last thing he needs to see is mom nude or barely dressed. A son cringes when thinking of his mom as a "normal woman" being pursued by men or having sex so he doesn't want to see his mom's body naked, nor lingerie dressed in any fashion. Of course, when your son is a baby, this doesn't apply but the moment you notice that your son is starting to stare or is being curious about your body (as a young child), it's time to cover up. To all the "no clothes wearing moms" I know it's hard but think about it like this- imagine if a dad walked around after getting out of the shower completely nude or just in underwear with everything accessible and was in the presence of his adolescent or teenage daughter. How would that be perceived?

In conclusion mom, again- your son is not yours. He came from and belongs to God. You were assigned the responsibility of raising, loving, and assisting him with fulfilling God's purpose for his life. Love but do not spoil him. Discipline but do not abuse him. Teach but do not belittle him. When he's older (a grown man), be his safe haven and his counselor when needed. There will come a time in his life when he just wants and needs to be comforted in trusting arms, arms that will not ridicule or judge. Normally those arms are the arms of a grandmother (because in grandma's eyes, he can do no wrong and her nurturing wisdom is extremely comforting) but mom, you can be those arms also. I once heard the rapper DMX say in an interview as he spoke about his grandmother, "every man wants to be a baby sometimes" and cried as he said this. Life can and will be hard at times and for men, we seldom have a safe place to go and have a "moment" without being looked upon as being weak. Be those welcoming arms that he can return to if needed. Arms that he can get out a good cry and then return to his normal self. But most importantly, be the navigator that points him in the direction of Gods path for his life because that's the ultimate mission that was assigned to you.

Now Mom, pass the book to your son and allow the real work to begin!

CHAPTER 2
PURPOSE

Young man if I was to ask you "who are you?" or "who do you hope to be?" what would you say? Before you answer, keep in mind this question doesn't pertain to your career goals or an aspiring dream. Becoming a Doctor, Lawyer, Athlete, Performer, Actor etc. are all professions (which is fine) but that doesn't necessarily say who you are. It's what you do or what you aspire to do. There's a road you must follow to achieve these goals so while you're on that road, who are you then? Who are you before you become that doctor, rapper, or athlete and who are you when you retire from that profession?

If you don't know the answer, it's okay. A lot of people don't know who they are. If you asked the average person, they would probably tell you what they do for a living but that doesn't necessarily say who they are. Most people haven't figured it out yet, some don't know they should, and others will never know. The reasoning behind this question is this; Discovering who you are or who you hope to become, leads you to the purpose for your life which was ordained by God.

Before your mother met your father, God had already made a plan for your life which is essentially your purpose for being born. You were designed by God, you're unique, you're special, one of a kind and you are here for a reason. God doesn't waist His time nor does he make any junk so no matter your circumstances are, you're a MIRICLE, and your life has significant value!

Discovering the purpose for your life will ultimately determine who you are. Now the million-dollar question is, how do you find your purpose? Instead of asking how, I suggest focusing on a better question which is "What's the process of finding your purpose?" Being as though you were born for a reason and that reason came from God, it only makes sense to find your purpose through God. One might ask, how? You find your purpose through God by having a personal one on one relationship with Him and staying connected to Him. Proverbs 3: 5-6 says "Trust in the LORD with all thine heart; And lean not unto thine own understanding. In all thy ways acknowledge Him, and he shall direct thy paths." It's a lot of life out here to be lived so while you're going through it, make and take the time to pray. Read His word. Talk to God. Stay connected to Him and eventually he will reveal your purpose to you.

Always keep in mind that your timing is not God's timing. In the bible, Moses didn't find his purpose till he was 80 years old. A lot of that had to do with Moses being stubborn which delayed his calling, but it didn't stop his purpose. Your purpose could be revealed to you at a very young age, or it could take years- maybe decades to be revealed. Be patient and stay connected to God. As you live your life, you will go through things, good, bad, and ugly- all to prepare you for your ultimate purpose which will define who you are.

You don't have to find, search, or look for your purpose. It will be revealed to you by God in His timing. You just have to stay connected to Him and pray and ask for wisdom so when He reveals it, you're able to know it's from Him and can receive it. So, in the meantime, live your life accordingly by setting goals and chasing your dreams. One of my favorite quotes goes as follows:

"Before you were born, God had a plan for your life. As time progressed, you developed a plan of your own. I pray that the two align."

-Dwayne Cooli Hi Jones

While in the moment you may think you're being who you're destined to be but with time, things can change. For example, if you could ask a young Fresh Prince (while he was rapping, going platinum and winning Grammys) if he was living in his purpose, he would probably say yes; not knowing that the actor Will Smith would follow and overshadow the rapper by a longshot and still may not be his ultimate purpose (only he and God knows). The young boxer Cassius Clay had no idea the activist and greatest athlete of all time Muhamad Ali would follow. More importantly the young Cassius Clay didn't have a clue that he would have to go through all of the turmoil outside of boxing to evolve into the person God designed him to ultimately be. For if he knew, he might have gone a different route. God purposely keeps the path a mystery, so we have to trust Him and go through the process. Wisdom is a gift from God so when He blesses you with it, you will know when your purpose has been revealed to you.

CHAPTER 3
EDUCATION

Growing up as a kid, I remember always hearing older folks say things like "Get a good education" or "Education is the key to a successful life." It was always a push to encourage students to stay in school and learn. Teachers and adults always emphasized how important a good education was, but they always left out the most important part, the missing piece to the puzzle. They left out the why.

Why is education so important? Why do adults push this narrative so hard? Social Studies, English, History, all these Math's- Algebra, Geometry, Calculus etc. why are these classes important? Why do you have to take these classes? What's the purpose if it doesn't tie directly into what you want to do with your life? Well son, I'm here to tell you why. There are three main reasons why education is important. Money, opportunity, and intellectual respect.

Money

Your education can or will determine how much money you will make as an adult- that simple. In most cases it will. Now of course there are a few one off's that you'll hear or read about when a high school dropout starts a business and becomes a millionaire, but these are one in a million odds. Majority of the time, the higher your education, the higher the pay when you enter the real world.

Statistics show (depending on the state you live in) high school dropouts (if employed) earn between 24K – 28K per year. High school graduates earn between 31K-37K per year. Thirty- seven thousand dollars a year comes out to roughly $770 per week ($3,083 a month). Now let's take a look at "basic" adult monthly expenses:

    Rent (in a decent neighborhood): $1,500 and up.
    Utilities (Light & Gas Bill): $150
    Cell Phone: $100
    Car Payment: $500
    Car Insurance (for a young adult): $300
    Groceries/ Toiletries: $250
    Home Internet: $50
    Gas: $240

TOTAL: $3,090

Please keep in mind, these numbers are general/ basic. They don't even include clothes, health insurance, outings (going on dates, hanging out with friends, etc.) subscriptions- fire sticks, PlayStation or Xbox. Generally, your monthly pay is $3,083 and your monthly basic expenses are at least $3,090. You will be living paycheck to paycheck, hand over fist, barely making it. God forbid if you get sick or injured and must miss time from work. Just the slightest bend from the norm and your living situation can be turned upside down. That's why in most cases, a high school diploma isn't enough. Now I'm not saying you can't have a good financial life with just a high school diploma. What I'm saying is with more than a high school diploma, you increase your chances of having better income.

For the dropouts- the ones without a high school diploma, your chances are very slim- next to none regarding financial stability. Hard manual labor, lots of lifting, cleaning and being on your feet constantly- basically physical labor would be the only option and for bare minimum pay.

After high school doesn't necessarily mean you have to go to college. College works for some but not all. There are so many dynamics regarding college, I could write a separate book on that topic alone from leaving home for the first time and living on campus to the financial cost- student loans, scholarships, financial aid (most importantly, paying it all back) but I won't go too deep down that rabbit hole. Let's just say college is an option but there are also other options such as trade schools.

There are so many trade school professions you can pursue in the Medical field, Mechanical field, Transportation (truck driving) Law Enforcement, Cybersecurity etc. The list goes on and on. Normally there's a cost to attend these trade schools (similar to college tuition) but you must do whatever's needed to obtain the desired skill. There's an old saying, "You can either pay now and play later or you can play now and pay later." What that means is while you're young, get all the schooling and training you need- (pay) so that later in life when you're older, you can kick back, relax, and enjoy the fruit that you harvested when you were younger- (play). But if you play while you're young by not getting the education or skills needed for future financial stability, I promise you're going to pay later in life.

The ultimate goal is to get a skill that someone will pay you the kind of money YOU need to live a life that avoids financial stress. You're the only one that truly knows what you're passionate about so if you have a passion that can lead to financial stability, I suggest that you pursue that goal at all costs. Making money for something that you love to do is bliss! When it's your true passion, you're basically getting paid for something you would do for free.

When your passion aligns with financial stability (and is achieved or achievable) consider yourself abundantly blessed. Sometimes our passions don't lead to financial stability. For example, someone could be passionate about art, music or some kind of sport but that doesn't necessarily mean they will become financially stable within one of these fields. It could happen but it also could not happen. Dream BIG and pursue your dreams at all costs, but also keep a plan B in your back pocket-just in case.

Think of higher education as an investment. If you're spending thousands of dollars and in most cases taking out loans for tuition or trade schools, at the end of the day you're going to want to see a return for all the money you borrowed and spent. That's why it's extremely important to choose a major or trade that guarantees as close as possible a well-paying profession after you graduate. Be careful not to choose a major or trade that doesn't convert into good pay. A lot of majors that tie into a passion don't "require" school. You can pursue some passions without school. Hard work, determination & drive is all you need. But if you're going to invest roughly 100K in school, it should be on major that leads to getting your money back plus more. It makes no sense to spend thousands of dollars for a degree in Art and then possibly be jobless after you graduate and in debt from the loans. Again, a lot of passion driven majors such as Art can be pursued minus college-minus $100K. There are lots of college graduates out here that have meaningless degrees which defeats the true purpose of getting the degree and that is to qualify for a good paying career.

Even if you're fortunate enough to land a job in corporate America (a corporation) you could possibly get stuck around the entry level without higher education. You will start to see new employees that were hired AFTER you, move up in the company, passing you, all because they have higher education credentials. Normally in cases like this, you will have to go back to school, all while you're now working and living an adult life just to enhance your career. That's why it's best to get as much schooling as you can BEFORE you jump out there into the real world. Get it over with while your brain is still young and fresh and before you have to deal with the challenges of being a full-grown adult.

The more education you have, the more money you can potentially make. There are always exceptions- most multi- millionaires (outside of sports) don't have college degrees but they are called exceptions for a reason. If you choose not to enhance your education, I pray that you are one of those exceptions. For the remaining majority, it should be a simple transaction between you and the college or trade school:

Dear Mr. College or Trade School- I will give you "X" amount of dollars (for tuition) in return for the knowledge and skill set to land a job or profession with financial security for life. It's basically that simple.

Opportunity

Education can and will open the flood gates to lots of opportunities also. For example, a kid growing up in a challenging environment (the ghetto) can use education to literally get them out of the hood. When a student excels at a high level at their zone public school (elementary) it's very possible that someone from the school will notice and normally that's when the suggestion of going to a better school comes into play. In the blink of an eye the student could possibly go from attending a school in his challenging environment to attending a school in a better neighborhood, with likeminded students and better education. Even if there's a cost- tuition, with excellent grades, school staff/ counselors will assist with finding financial resources- funding and the kid could possibly be sponsored all the way through high school- hence removing the student from the challenging environment and placing them in a better environment- all from education.

This scenario doesn't have to start from elementary school. It can start from any grade from 1-12 and even more commonly after high school. That's where scholarships come in to play. Typically, when young male students think of scholarships, they think of sports but actually there are more students receiving academic scholarships than athletic scholarships. Graduating from high school with high honors could possibly earn a full paid scholarship at a college which again removes a student from a challenging environment and taking them to a place mom and dad could never afford financially. Perfect examples of how education provides opportunities and can take you places you couldn't imagine being without having money.

Education also enhances the opportunity for you to grow in any desired field you choose as a young adult. I often hear a lot of young men say that they want to start their own business. They don't want to work for anyone. They want to be their own boss. But the question you must ask yourself is- how? Do you know the infrastructure of business? Do you know what's required from the state you reside in regarding documents as well as the financial cost? Do you know what line of business you want to pursue and is it profitable?

In most cases, you must be taught these things. Sure, you can google a lot of information but it's nothing like having someone take you under their wing and showing you firsthand. That person would be a mentor and in lots of cases, mentors notice and reach out to young men with potential.

Successful businessmen/women like to surround themselves with smart people. Now please don't confuse being smart with having an education. There are a lot of people that obtained a great education but are not the smartest- but they were smart ENOUGH to know how a good education could enhance their life financially. Then there are the smartest young men out there without education that could run circles around the ones who have it. The only problem is, it's hard for them to get noticed because they are not in the same company with the educated- which leads back to how education provides opportunities and places you in rooms that are difficult to get in without it.

Intellectual Respect

The third and final point I want to speak on is how education can earn you intellectual respect. This is where all the classes you took such as Algebra, History, English etc. come into play. Although you may not directly use what was learned in these classes in your future profession, it's very possible that you'll indirectly use what was learned daily. These classes will make you knowledgeable and knowledge is POWER.

Knowledge is power- another cliche but what does that saying exactly mean? It means when you have knowledge, you're not easily swayed to believe anything someone "tells" you because you're able to think and make decisions on your own. It means you're able to decipher a truth from a lie and no one can take advantage of your mind (in certain situations). It means when you speak, you know what you're talking about so your words have meaning. It means you simply know things and you're not just wandering around in the dark.

** Note: Knowledge is power, but INFORMATION is powerful! Knowledge consists of knowing things, but information is the key that unlocks ALL doors.

Being fluent in subjects like History, Math, Science etc. will also open opportunities for intellectual conversations which ultimately gains you intellectual respect. Have you ever received a text message from someone or read a post on social media where the grammar was incorrect, or some words were spelled wrong? Depending on how bad the message was (sometimes it could be typo's) you probably subconsciously judged the sender's intellect. If you haven't, it's possible that you're the sender!

Whether you know it or not, people are judged by others from what they know (education) because it's comes out in how they read, write, or speak. Knowing when to use "you're" vs. "your" or "there" vs. "their" is important. If you've never heard of Sigmund Freud or don't know what REM sleep is, chances are you didn't take Psych 101 (a standard college course) which also means your education probably stopped at high school.

Your level of education can sometimes determine how well you write, speak, and comprehend what you read. Your level of education can also determine how well you hold up in certain conversations- all which leads to intellectual respect.

When you're well educated, you're able to speak on and understand a wide variety of topics. Hardly any conversations will "go over your head" or make you feel uncomfortable. Education broadens your horizon. You'll be able to speak on topics from the latest news in the hood to the key battles of the Civil War back in 1861 (without google).

Life is harder without education. Again, there are many advantages of having a good education, but my top three are Money, Opportunity, and Intellectual Respect. Another gem to keep a hold of is no matter how much education you have, always thirst for more. Not necessarily degrees and accolades but more so, information and knowledge. Be a sponge everywhere you go- quick to listen and comprehend and slow to speak, ensuring your words have adequate meaning. Always remember, you don't always have to know things, you just have to know where to go to find the answers.

CHAPTER 4
FINANCE

Back when I was coming up, conversations about money were always sensitive. As kids we were always taught not to disclose how much money we had because someone might try to take our money or con us out of it. Money was a private matter- a secret. Regarding adults, financial responsibilities were never discussed with children. It was considered "grown folks' business".

In today's time some of that still applies. Everyone shouldn't know your financial details however young men such as yourself should be able to discuss money with experienced adults so you can understand money, how it works and how to make good financial decisions.

Since financial responsibilities were never discussed with children, when growing up we were never taught how to manage money- how to pay bills, the difference between renting, leasing and owning, the importance of credit scores etc. We had to figure these things out as we lived. Again, an entire separate book could be written on these topics alone, but I'll just highlight a few major points that I believe are important to know. For starters, it is important for you to know that money isn't REAL. I'll repeat- MONEY IS NOT REAL. Here's why I say this:

Some years ago, I was on a flight headed to Los Angeles leaving from Baltimore. Prior to boarding the plane, I had accidentally packed my wallet in one of my suitcases which was checked and boarded on the plane. I only had my ID and some cash in my pockets. I figured I would be okay because I had cash in my pocket just in case I wanted some food while in flight. I could retrieve my wallet once we landed.

While in mid-flight, the flight attendant began to walk the aisle taking food and drink orders. I was hungry and decided I would order something to eat. I placed my order, reached in my pocket, and attempted to hand the flight attendant a fifty-dollar bill to pay for my food. The flight attendant then looked at me and said "I'm sorry sir but we don't accept cash. We only accept credit or debit cards."

That was the very moment when I realized money wasn't real. You see, it didn't matter to the flight attendant that I had enough "money" to pay for the food or not. Money wasn't being accepted. Only credit or debit cards. Although I had money to pay, I couldn't get any food while on the plane.

That experience taught me that the only thing anyone can do with money is trade it for something they REALLY want. On that flight, I was hungry and wanted food. I couldn't eat the fifty-dollar bill. I could only exchange it for what I really wanted and that was food. The same concept applies to everything we need or want. When we are cold, money can't keep us warm. We exchange money for a coat, a blanket or the heat that blows out of our vents. We can't eat money. We can't wear money. We can't drive or live in money. Money is the middleman. We only need it so we can exchange it for something and that's all we can do with it. Nothing else. We can only exchange/ spend it. Even if we save it till the day we pass away, eventually it will get passed along and someone else will exchange/ spend it.

So when I say money isn't real, what I mean is what's really real are the clothes that are on your back, the car you drive, the house you live in, etc. Money was just the pathway to get these things. When your life is over, you can't take it with you. You can only give it to someone else so that they can exchange it for what they really want.

With that being said, don't make money your end all be all- meaning don't make money your God. Money is very important and is needed to live a sustainable lifestyle but always know that it's just a pathway to your true needs and wants. When you're thirsty you want/ need water- not a 5-dollar bill. The 5-dollar bill allows you to buy the water but if you had another way of getting the water, the 5-dollar bill isn't needed. The moment the person or store that has the water decides that money isn't the trade off, the 5-dollar bill is now worthless.

1 Timothy 6:10 says "For the love of money is a root of all kinds of evil." Not money but the LOVE of money. That's very important to know.

Since money is the pathway to obtaining practically all of life's tangible "things", it's extremely important for you to know how to manage money. There are so many key components regarding money that you should know but the first topic I want to bring your way is credit.

In my opinion, credit is the most crucial part of financial literacy there is. It's mind blowing to me that this isn't mandatory to be taught in all schools because it's such a vital part of everything regarding finances when you become an adult.

For those of you who don't know what credit is or may have heard the term used loosely, credit just means a legal promise. A financial institution- a bank, credit union or some kind of lender, loans you money and you're legally promising to pay them back. Here's how it works.

A vast majority of the world is run by credit which is essentially a loan. Large companies hardly ever pay for things in full. They usually take on partners (to share the risk just in case things don't work out as planned) or a line of credit which would be a loan. The overall idea is to keep as much of your own money in your pocket and make moves with other people's/ investors (or the banks) money which generally defines business.

In my freshman year of college, I remember walking across campus and being swayed by a credit card representative to come over to their table and apply for their card. I had no idea how credit worked at that time. I always saw people in movies and on TV pull out credit cards to pay for things, but I didn't understand how it worked. Needless to say, I was swayed to apply and was approved! Why would a bank give a 17–18-year-old college freshman with no source of income (a job) a credit card still baffles me, but they did.

A little over a week later I received the card in the mail. The limit on the credit card was $300. Me not understanding credit nor how it worked thought I had a free $300! I went to the mall, bought clothes, shoes etc.

and ordered pizza almost every night. Within 3 days, I maxed out the entire credit card (spent the $300).

A little over a month later, I received a bill requesting for my first payment. I was broke and couldn't pay the bill. Even if I had some money and could have paid it, I wouldn't because I wasn't financially mature enough to do so. I probably would have bought more clothes and food. Again, I didn't understand how credit worked so I ignored the bill.

Over the next couple of months more and more bills started to come, and I continued to ignore them. The $300 initial bill had almost doubled due to late and interest fees. More time passed and eventually the bank closed the credit line/ card with me owing a little over $600. Still, this didn't bother me at all. My life was not altered in any way.

Fast forwarding to a few years later, I'm now sitting in a car dealership attempting to purchase my first car. After negotiating the final price for the car, the car salesman sent me to the financing department at the dealership to finalize the deal. Again, all of this was new to me. The finance department asked for my social security number so they could check my credit. The young lady that was handling the financing returned after checking my credit and said, "I'm sorry but we can't approve this loan".

What I didn't know was that credit card I had back in my freshman year of college came back to haunt me. When I ignored and didn't pay that credit card bill, that bank told every bank/ lender in the entire country (USA) what I did. It's called a credit score. So now when I'm attempting to get another loan- for a car this time, I'm now getting denied.

Before any bank/ lender approves you for a loan, the first thing they'll do is check to see if you have any old loans that haven't been paid, if you have current loans and are they up to date, and if you have a history of paying your bills late or on time. Again, it's called checking your credit score. The higher your credit score, the more you are likely to be approved for loans. The lower the score, the more likely you'll have a higher interest rate (which means if you borrow $10,000, you'll have to pay $13,000 back- compared to others that may only have to pay $11,000 back) or denied.

That's why credit is so important. To buy a car, credit is needed. To rent an apartment, credit is needed. To buy a house, credit is needed and even some jobs check your credit before hiring you!

A quick example of how credit/ loans come into play is the process of buying a car. Let's say you go to a car dealership, pick out a car and the car cost $30,000. If you don't have $30,000 in your pocket or in a bank account to give to the car dealership, you will not be driving away with that car. Since the average person isn't walking around with $30,000 in their pocket, a loan is necessary. The finance department at the dealership will then try to find a bank/ lender that would be willing to loan you the $30,000. When searching for a bank/ lender to loan you the money, guess what's the first thing they're going to check? Your credit history! Your credit score, how much money you're making on your job, along with many other factors will decide whether they will approve your loan. If approved, the bank will give the dealership the $30,000, you will get the keys and drive off and now you owe the bank $30,000 plus the interest fees (that's how the bank makes money). Depending on your credit score, you could have to pay anywhere from $32,000 - $39,000 back. The bank will break down the total amount owed into monthly payments, and this is what adults refer to as car payments. If all goes well, after 6 years (72 months) of making these payments, the car is officially yours! But if you miss several payments, the bank has the right to take the car back and you will lose the previous monthly payments you made along with still owing the bank for the car.

Note: I left out a lot of minor details in this process for the purpose of keeping this as simple as possible.

The same for buying a house. If approved, the bank gives the person or business that's selling the house the money- let's say $250,000 and you now owe the bank that money in return plus interest- but instead of 6 years, a house is normally a 30-year process. It's called a mortgage.

When renting an apartment, the property owner will want to know if they can depend on you to pay your rent and pay it on time, so they check your credit also. Again, this is why credit is so important.

As for you, a young man soon to be entering adulthood, chances are you don't have any credit at all (no loans attached to your name). Establishing your credit is a must but you shouldn't apply for any credit/ loans until you're financially ready. The best thing to do when you're young is to ask your mom, dad, or a close relative to add you as an "Authorized User" to their credit cards. This will allow you to build your credit while you're young without having to make payments yourself.

When you do become of age and have financial maturity, always pay your bills on time to ensure your credit rating stays in good standing. Also, do not ignore and not pay any bills you create because that could lead to your present or future pay being garnished. Garnishment means a creditor with the approval of the courts, can be granted permission to take their money directly from your paycheck that your job issues you BEFORE you receive it. If a garnishment is issued against you, whoever you owe will be allowed to take up to 25% of your paycheck every week until they receive the total amount owed.

If you decide to have credit cards, try your best not to exceed over 1/3 of the credit limit. For example, if you're given a line of credit on a card in the amount of $1,000, try not to use more than $333 of the $1,000. Paying your bills on time along with your card utilization (your balance compared to how much is available for spending), all contributes to how your credit score is calculated.

Another important thing to know is how to manage your money- what to buy and what not to buy. In my lifetime, I've witnessed so many people have access to large amounts of money but didn't know how to manage it which caused them to lose it. If someone gave you a million dollars today, without money managing skills, chances are you will be broke within a year. That's why knowing how to manage money is so important.

There are two key words that you must know regarding money that will determine whether you're going to be a successful manager of your money. Those two words are assets and liabilities.

Liabilities are things that lose value after you buy them. Examples of liabilities are clothes, shoes, and most cars. When you buy any of the items just mentioned-the very moment after you purchase it, it immediately loses value. If you own a pair of jeans or some sneakers and decided to sell them, these items are considered as used so you probably won't get the same amount back compared to what you paid for them. That's what makes them liabilities. If you were to buy a brand-new car today, the moment you drove the car of the lot, the car's value would immediately drop. Anything you can think of that after you own it and decide you want to sell it but will not bring back at least the amount you paid for it, is a liability.

Assets are things that hold or gain value after you buy them. Examples of assets are houses, land, gold, and some equipment. When you buy any of these items mentioned there's a very slim chance that you will lose money and a very high chance that you will gain money when or if you ever decide to sell. If you bought a house for $100,000 you could later sell that same house for $150,000 (more or less). One thing for sure is you will not lose money when selling an asset. Anything that you can think of that after you buy it, you can later sell it (if you choose to) for either equal to or more than you paid for it, is considered to be an asset.

Note: If you're wondering where would you get $100,000 to buy a house, well that's when all of the previous topics in this book comes into play. From the Education leading to a substantial financial career to the most important part we just discussed- credit.

The key to managing your money is to buy and own more assets than liabilities. Although liabilities lose value, in life you're going to have and need some of them, but the key is to not have more liabilities than assets. Owning more liabilities than assets is a guaranteed road to the poor house. Spend your money on things that if you had to sell, would bring the money you paid for it back or possibly even more money. Surrounding yourself with assets guarantees that you'll never be broke! Assets increase your money. Liabilities take away from your money.

So when you have money or get access to money, don't waste it on clothes, shoes, cars, eating out at five-star restaurants etc. Focus more on land, property, investments, anything that will hold its value and possibly give you more money than what you paid for it. ROI- return on investment is a term you want to be very familiar with. The clothes, shoes and cars etc. (liabilities) should come AFTER the assets are in place but they should NEVER outweigh your assets.

Here are three other gems regarding money that you might find helpful in the future.

1. Do not rent if possible. Own. But if you do have to rent (which we all have done or had to do at some point in our lives), do so in the shortest time frame as possible. Renting is basically throwing money away-

especially if it's for a long period of time. You're paying for something that isn't yours and will never be. They're so many financial advantages available to you when you own/ buy a home, again I could write a separate book on. When you initially move out for the first time and live on your own, chances are you'll be renting but just know that it should be temporary and short term as possible.

2. Never keep all your money in one place. Always have and maintain several bank accounts. When you get paid from your job, set up a direct deposit specifically for that transaction alone. This will be your main account- pay from your job to this specific account only. Do not use this account for ANYTHING ELSE. Open or set up a separate account to pay your bills, get gas, shop etc. The reason for this is to keep your main account isolated so there's a slim chance of someone getting access to it- whether it be a hack or some charge or penalty from the bank or a collector. Isolating your main account ensures that no other entity can touch your real money. You can transfer whatever you need to the other accounts to pay bills or do whatever you desire and if something was to happen to your secondary accounts, the damage won't be as severe as it would be if it hit your main account.

Also, set up a miscellaneous account and keep a bare minimum in it for purchases like swiping your card at small gas stations, carry out food or vending machines. There are some places that you might not feel comfortable with using your card because of the risk of being hacked so you use your miscellaneous card at these places. Keep a small amount of money in this account so if it's hacked, the hacker will not get any real money. No more than $50 should be in this account.

3. If you ever decide to lend someone money, always follow this rule. Only lend an amount of money that you can afford to lose. Meaning, do not lend an amount of money that if the person you're lending it to doesn't pay you back when they said they would or even pay you back at all, that the amount of money you loaned them won't affect your finances in a negative way. You choose the amount by assuming that you're GIVING it to them- sort of like a gift. That way, if they don't pay you back, it doesn't affect your finances but if they do pay you back, it's a plus because in your mind you weren't expecting it back anyway. Having to depend on money that you loaned out being paid back puts you in a very vulnerable state and often leads to conflict. The best approach is to lend a comfortable amount and don't expect to be paid back (but don't tell the person you're lending to that- of course). That's an agreement between you and you!

Also, never double loan. If you loan someone money and they didn't pay you back, you should never loan them a second loan (until they pay the first one back). If they couldn't pay the first loan, chances are slim to none that they'll pay both loans back so save yourself the headache.

If you haven't already, one day you'll hear or read about people hitting the lottery for millions of dollars or athletes that made millions ending up broke. The reason for this is because it doesn't matter how much money you make or have, if you don't know how to manage it, you will lose it.

Everything discussed thus far are just a few tips on money management and how finances work. As with everything I would advise you to continue to seek knowledge on financial literacy by reading books, having conversations with financial experts, and studying successful people with money. Always remember to never make money your God because if so, no amount will ever be enough. Don't chase money. Use money- use it to exchange it for whatever your heart desires but also manage it correctly so it works for YOU instead of YOU working for it!

CHAPTER 5
The Importance of Relationships

We've touched a lot of important subjects so far from finding your purpose, to the importance of education and also understanding how money works but there's another topic that puts the icing on the cake that we've been baking since the beginning of the read. That topic is RELATIONSHIPS. Outside of the spiritual and your connection with God, understanding relationships is the most important piece of life's puzzle because it ties together everything that we've discussed, with a red bow!

The biggest false statement that I've ever heard was hearing people say, "I don't need anyone" or "I can do this all by myself". These statements only apply on the small scale when measuring personal/ self-goals such as self-motivation, preparing yourself for a particular task or taking care of yourself in some way but on a larger scale these statements do not apply at all. In life, we all will need somebody. It may not be a specific person, but we will need someone in some way. When we're connected to God, that someone is who God uses as a vessel to deliver HIS blessings. I once heard a joke that goes:

"One day there was a man drowning in the water. A boat comes by and says do you need any help? The man says no thank you. God will save me. Then another boat came by and asked the same- do you need any help. The man replied again, no thanks- God will save me. The man drowned and when he got to heaven, he asked God why didn't you save me? God replied- I sent you two boats!"

God doesn't come to you in the physical form (as a human being) so what HE will do is use people as a vessel, a message or blessing deliverer to bless you. That's why it's extremely important to stay connected to God so HE can bless you with wisdom so you can determine who HE sent to you from the bad seeds that are used by the devil.

Note: If you're not sure who's who, don't worry. God has a way of using your enemies to bless you also. What the devil designed for bad, God will use for good. Just believe, trust and stay connected to God and He will direct your paths.

When it comes to relationships, the most important one to have is with God. If you're wondering how to build or have a relationship with God, it's very simple. Spend time with HIM. Read His word (the Bible). Pray and talk to Him. God is a person (a spiritual person). There is no right or wrong way to talk to Him. Like all relationships, the more time you spend, the stronger the relationship will be.

When your relationship with God is intact, all healthy and meaningful relationships that follow will be an extension of your relationship with Him. God will purposely bring people into your life to bless you so it's important for you to know how to navigate and build relationships with others.

In life, you will meet all kinds of people through different channels but generally we all meet most people we know in similar ways. As a kid, most of the people that you'll meet will probably be from school, the neighborhood in which you grew up in, an extracurricular activity such as sports or a particular hobby or community activities such as church or other organizations. When you get older, you'll meet more people in college or trade school, social gatherings or on your job. These are the basic general pools the average person has to choose from regarding meeting people. Depending on your personality, this pool can either expand or shrink. An extrovert (an outgoing person) may meet new people everywhere they go while an introvert (someone that stays to themselves) may not associate with people in their general pool so they probably won't meet new people in other places either.

Stemming from the general pool, in the early stage of your life, your social class (your neighborhood) and your education (the people you went to school with) will determine the people you'll meet and have relationships with. Circling back to education, that's why it's important because your education could possibly change the environment of the people you attend school with which also changes the people you'll have relationships with.

For example- Picture a scenario with two young boys- one born living in the inner city of a rough neighborhood and the other in a high-class suburban area. The inner-city boy will go to school and socialize with other kids from that environment and although they maybe good people- chances are they won't have as many resources as others. When the boy builds relationships with his other inner city peers and goes to visit one of his friends, the mother of the friend may not be home because she's at work and the father (if he's still around) might be into "other things" and might not be the best role model for the boys.

Note: Again an entire separate book can be written as to why this is in our inner city black families-

SYSTEMATICALLY, but I'll save that for another time.

Now with the boy born and raised in the high class suburban area, he will go to school and build relationships in his environment also. The major difference is, he will probably have more RESOURCES than the inner-city boy. When he visits his friends, chances are he'll see what a family should look like. The father might be a CEO at some company that can later in life hire the boy, advise him, or recommend him to another company but most importantly the boy actually sees what "success" looks like- compared to the inner-city boy that doesn't have a clue. The suburban young man will have access to resources from job and career opportunities to entrepreneurial-ship and money tips, while the inner city young man has to try his best to figure things out on his own- which can be done but just a more difficult task.

No one can control the environment they're born into but it's important to understand your circumstances so you can move accordingly. For the inner-city boy, education can literally take you from one scenario to another and place in a circle full of resources. But even higher than education, a connection with GOD trump's everything because GOD can and will place you in rooms and around people that you couldn't even imagine- even when you're not worthy or qualified. It's called Gods favor- having His GRACE. You just have to stay connected to Him.

Always remember- "WHO you know will get you there but WHAT you know will keep you there."- Dwayne "Cooli Hi' Jones

During the time that I'm writing this book, Bronny James (Lebron James's son) has just been drafted to the NBA (Los Angeles Lakers). WHO Bronny knew (his father) got him there but WHAT he knows (the hard work and sacrifices he made and will continue to do so) will keep him there (if it's God's will). The same applies for the average person. Who you know may get your foot in the door whether it be a career or some sort of opportunity but what you know will keep you there and allow you to grow.

Nepotism is a common practice in today's society.

Note: If you don't know what Nepotism means, look it up (google it). Some things I'll say in this reading will be very understandable and some will not. There's an underlying goal here and that is to challenge and push your hunt for knowledge.

Depending on your situation you could benefit from nepotism, or you could be impacted by it. Whichever way the chips may fall, it's important to build and sustain strong relationships wherever you go to either combat nepotism or make it make sense and here are a few tips on how to do so.

Father Figure

1. Be respectful to all. Treat everyone the same (like you would want to be treated). Treat the janitor at the multimillion-dollar company the exact same way you would treat the CEO. Treat the homeless person on the street the same way you would treat the President of the United States. Outside of the cliche sayings like "the same people you see going up are the same people you'll see coming down" and "be careful not to burn bridges you may need to cross again later", it's morally the right thing to do.

2. As children we all were taught not to talk to strangers (for safety reasons) but when you become an adult, that concept goes out of the window. Talk to as many strangers as possible because your inner circle might actually be a square, boxing you in and prohibiting you from growing and reaching your full potential. There's an old saying that goes "If you're the smartest person in the room, you're in the wrong room!" What that means is if you're the smartest in the room, who can you turn to when in need of advice or information? Surround yourself with people that you aspire to be like, as much as possible.

The whole notion of "no new friends" and "stick with you day ones (friends you grew up with or have had for a long time)" is bull crap. Living by these sayings puts a cap on your network and depending on who your "day one" friends are, could hold you back from your full potential. Keep your "day ones" but don't limit yourself to just one group of people. Talk to new people and be open to have random conversations with strangers. You never know- that stranger could be an angel in disguise sent by God to bless you!

Expand and travel when necessary. Depending on your goals or purpose in life, where you were born or raised may not be the best place for you to grow. You may have to move to a different city, state or even another country. Who you're destined to be maybe too large for the city you were born in. More resources and opportunities may be elsewhere. Don't limit or suppress who you are just because you want to stay close to friends and family. Responsibilities, yes but family and friends no. You can always come back and visit. Go wherever you need to go, meet new people and build new relationships if the city you're born in doesn't align with your life goals.

When you build relationships, essentially, you're building your network. The more meaningful relationships you have the bigger your network will be which translates to more resources for you to have access to. The world we live in revolves heavily on relationships. Majority of the time hard work and dedication isn't enough. It's going to take meeting the right people or person to help elevate you to where you want to be. When in the mists of any gathering of people, be slow to speak and quick to listen to identify positive opportunities but also to avoid bad situations. Pray and ask God to bring the right people into your life and to warn you of the wrong. Build relationships with others as much as possible but be careful not to confuse relationships with friendships.

FRIENDSHIPS

As previously stated, you will meet lots of people over the course of your life but very few will be considered and called a friend. Friends are people who you share the same interests and values with, people that are loyal and trustworthy, people that will never let any harm come your way, and people you can trust with your deepest darkest secrets and will have your back till the end of time- no matter what. In life, consider yourself lucky if you're blessed to have ONE friend. You'll have a lot of associates, acquaintances, and seasonal friends but true friends are very hard to come by. To have a friend you must first know how to be a friend.

Knowing how to be a friend enables you to identify friendship characteristics in others and it also allows you to set expectations for yourself for others to qualify as a friend. When you yourself have these characteristics, you'll know what to expect from others. Here are a few important characteristics of being a good friend.

1. Being able to have and show EMPATHY. Empathy is simply removing all pre assumptions you may have about someone and viewing things from their perspective. It's seeing a situation from someone else's point of view- putting yourself in their shoes. Without empathy it's almost impossible to have any form of a healthy relationship yet alone a friendship. Having empathy for others allows you to guard your actions and your words- so you're not quick to judge, which makes it probably the most important characteristic of a friendship.

2. Be a good listener. Majority of the time when someone is venting- meaning, telling you what's going on specifically about an issue they're dealing with, they don't necessarily want or need advice or a rebuttal at that time. What they need is an ear to listen. Someone to not necessarily agree but understand their point of view. If they're saying something that needs correction, make a mental note and circle back later AFTER the person has finished venting. Being a good listener shows a person that you really care about them. A not so good friend listens with the intent to find a point to argue, criticize or combat but a true friend listens for one purpose only and that is to UNDERSTAND.

3. Tell hard truths with care. Being a "yes man" (a person that agrees with EVERYTHING just to stay on good terms with someone) is just as bad as being the

persons enemy. Real friends are honest with each other. Even if the truth is a painful truth, it should still be told because omitting the truth or lying (fearing the truth will jeopardize the friendship) will only lead to disasters later down the road. Also, never say anything about a friend behind their back that you are not willing to say to their face.

Friendships aren't usually sort after. They just organically happen. As I stated earlier, you'll meet all kinds of people in the course of your life. In most cases, you'll have seasonal friends that may not appear to be seasonal at the time. A seasonal friend is a friendship that only last for a short period of time. That's why it's called a "season". For example, in elementary school you and a person (or persons) could be the best of friends- inseparable, always together laughing and having fun from kindergarten all the way to the 5th grade. Then "life" happens, and you go to different middle schools or move into different neighborhoods or cities. You guy's attempt to stay in contact as much as possible but you all are now on separate roads of your lives, exploring new interest, meeting new friends, and essentially growing apart. Fast forward- a few years later you may come across one another and be happy to see each other, reminiscing about the past but in all actuality depending on how much you've stayed in contact over the years, you really don't know each other anymore.

You both know the kid from the past. That would be a seasonal friend- kindergarten through 5th grade.

Then there are times when you simply outgrow someone. You and a person could be good friends at a particular time in your life but when you start evolving and your friend doesn't, the friendship usually fades and that once a friend turns into an associate. If the friendship completely ends, it would be considered seasonal.

Outgrowing friends can be uncomfortable but necessary. In life, nothing that's alive ever stays the same. People are constantly changing, evolving, and growing. In your life, as you grow whether it's mentally, financially, or spiritually some of your friends may not be growing at the same pace as you or growing in reverse- which means not growing at all. In cases like this although it may be hard, you must cut ties with some because that friend or those friends may not be in Gods plans for the next chapters of your life. We all like what's familiar because it's comfortable but sometimes we must step out of our comfort zones to advance and move forward. Leaving some friends behind can sometimes be a part of that process.

Please know that there is nothing wrong with seasonal friends. Some seasonal friends are longer or shorter than others and a lot of times create the BEST memories. But if you're lucky, some or maybe one or two of these friends that you make during the course of your life will be there through ALL seasons- whether if you transfer to a different school, move to a different location, get a new job- no distance or circumstance will be able to alter the friendship. These people or this person would be who you consider to be a true friend.

Girls & Relationships

When it comes to girls and relationships, one could never cover every detail so what I'll do is cover the major points and then allow the GREATEST TEACHER ON EARTH to cover the rest- EXPERIENCE. All relationships are case by case- meaning each one can have its own uniqueness. All girls are different but at the same time they are the same. The only thing that will be constant in every relationship you'll be involved in is YOU so let's start there.

The most difficult part of talking to girls is actually building up the nerves to talk to girls. There's no magic trick that will help but what I would recommend for starters, is to get comfortable with just speaking to girls by saying hi. Every girl you come across, just say hi and leave at that. The more you do so, the more comfortable you'll become and soon after, conversations will begin. Greetings are important. When you start off by saying hi, what's up, how are you doing or whatever wording you use to greet her, you should be able to read her response to determine if it's going to be a difficult or easy conversation moving forward. Being able to read a girl's tone, facial expressions and body language is an important skill to have but again this comes with experience. The more you interact with girls the better you'll get at it. Once you have this skill you'll be able to shift your conversation if necessary according to the vibe you're getting. Almost like a boxing match- you'll be able to see when and where to throw punches (by reading the pattern of your opponent) in order to score points.

Also you have to have tough skin. You can't be overly sensitive. Rejection is a part of the game. You can't be afraid of the word "NO". You're probably going to hear that word from girls 10 times more than you'll hear YES. The key is to keep pursuing- not necessarily the same girl but different girls. Also never be afraid to approach the "unapproachable girl"- the baddest, prettiest girl of them all. Think about it like this- she's going to date someone, why not you!? You make HER tell you no. You NEVER say no to yourself (that's what you do if you don't approach her at all).

Depending on your personality, talking to girls can be the most nerve wracking thing in the world to do. You may start sweating, your stomach might turn in knots with butterflies, your thoughts might go blank, and you might even stutter when speaking. All of these things are normal in the beginning when you first start interacting with girls but good news- as you get older and the more you do it, it becomes a lot easier.

**Some boys with more outgoing personalities don't experience any of these things at all. Approaching and talking to girls comes easy to them but these guys are exceptions to the process.

Unfortunately there isn't a blueprint on what to initially say to a girl when approaching her. You just have to jump in the water and attempt to swim. You're probably going to say some "not too cool" things in the beginning but as you continue to approach girls, you'll figure out what works for you.

There are many different approaches you can use- some guys use humor (being funny). Others use romance (attempting to sweep her off her feet). The ultimate goal is to make her smile. When you're able to make a girl laugh or smile it lowers any wall she may have that's guarding her access. The more she smiles, the lower the wall becomes. Whatever approach you use, make sure it fits your personality because if you fake it, it will be obvious and noticeable. But no matter what you say or what approach you take, you must have the most important trait of them all which is CONFIDENCE.

Without confidence nothing will work. Girls like guys that are sure of themselves. Not cocky but confident. If you're not sure of yourself, why would anyone else be? Timidness is not attractive to girls because they won't ever feel completely safe in that guy's presence. Girls want to feel safe so you must always provide that security and it starts with confidence. When speaking, especially to other guys in her presence, speak with authority and look the guy straight in the eye. If shaking hands, make sure the handshake is firm.

** Outside of girls- this is a general rule. Speaking with authority and eye contact shows anyone that you're greeting you're confident and sure of yourself and you're not intimidated by their presence. Another male or any person should never have to ask you to repeat yourself because you're speaking too soft, and they can't hear you. That's a sign of weakness. Even if you're not sure, say it like you are!

Circling back to confidence as it relates to girls, confidence assures girls that they can believe in your actions and what you're saying. Almost anything said or done with confidence is somewhat believable. That's why when dealing with girls, everything must be fueled with confidence.

Understand this- most men are naturally hunters. We must go after everything we want in life. No one freely gives a man anything. If someone does freely give us something, often we don't want it. We are organically charged by going after things. It's the thrill of going after something and getting it that pushes us. Competition and winning. That's why sports play such a dominant role in our lives. We'll compete in everything from sports to who can toss a paper ball into a small trash can. We're just wired that way.

Circling back to girls, if you're interested in her, well there's probably about ten other guys interested in her also. So, you must do everything in your power to get her to choose you over the other guys. "How do I do that" you might ask? Again, there's no magical words or a secret code to use to get a girl to like you. You're going to have to figure out your own unique style of approaching (and a lot of times that comes with experience- the more you talk to girls, the better you'll get at it). Each scenario can be different. But here are a few general pointers that will get you going in the right direction.

1. Let's start with your appearance. Keep yourself up to par. Your hair should be kept up- neat with a fresh shape up (as much as possible). Brush your teeth, floss and use a tongue scraper. Make sure your breath smells good (use breath mints if necessary). This is MAJOR when it comes to girls. They HATE bad oral hygiene. Keep your clothes as clean and neat as possible. Depending on your age, you may not have a choice of what clothes

you have but you can control whether if they're clean- Especially your shoes or sneakers. Take showers- never smell musty. Always keep your skin moisturized- never ashy and always smell good by using cologne.

Stay fresh and clean but don't overdo it. Girls don't like guys that are in the mirror more than them. If you're at the age of having company whether it be your room, dorm, or apartment, keep your place clean and smelling good by slightly spraying your pillows with cologne. By doing these things you automatically separate yourself from a lot of guys which gives you at least a slight advantage. A clean environment represents order and when things are organized and in order, not only girls but all people organically feel safe. For example, picture two neighborhoods- one clean with beautiful trees, birds chirping, single family homes with two door garages and an occasional jogger passing by. Then picture the other with trash all over the sidewalk and street, rotten trees barely standing and people standing on the corner talking loudly. Which neighborhood would you feel safer in? When people feel safe, they are more likely to relax and the more a girl feels relaxed, the lower her resistance. Cleanliness is comforting to girls and the more a girl feels comfortable around you, the better the chance for you to connect with them.

2. Invest time and effort in getting to generally know girls. Study them. Get familiar with what they generally

like and dislike. Again, all girls are different but still the same. Watch and listen to them. Pay attention to their patterns and behaviors with the intention of not to manipulate or take advantage, but to understand them.

Remember girls are wired differently than boys. Girls are generally emotionally driven while boys are logically driven. So, a lot of their actions are based on how they feel. How a person feels can change in the blink of an eye therefore so can a girl's perception of any situation at any given time. In addition to being emotionally driven, girls have hormones and monthly cycles that affect how they feel which in turn can alter their moods at times. Being familiar with how girls are wired will help you understand when a girl says she's hungry but doesn't know what she wants to eat or when she's talking about one thing, switches and talks about another and in a split-second, talk about a third thing. From a guy's logical point of view, you might think their actions at times (especially when emotions are high) are crazy but they're not. They're just projecting what they FEEL at that particular moment.

Familiarize yourself with the things that girls generally like and are in to. This can be done simply by paying close attention to all girls and women and make mental notes on what they all generally like and have in common. For example, some girls may like roses- some may not. But the key here is, for the ones that don't like roses- figuring out the replacement. It could be handwritten cards, teddy bears, balloons etc. The ultimate goal is to make her happy, to make her smile so whether if it's roses or fingernail polish, your objective is to figure it out and provide. Uncovering a girl's key to happiness (without her having to tell you) is almost a guaranteed in.

3. Respect all girls (even if they don't respect themselves) and provide a general form of protection for them. Don't let anyone harm a female in your presence. Open and hold doors for them. Never sit while a girl stands. Offer her your seat. If she declines, still stand, and leave the seat vacant just in case she changes her mind. When or if you're old enough to drive, open the car door for her and close it after she's seated.

Do not hit or physically harm girls in any way, shape, or form but at the same time, do not sit back and allow a girl to physically harm you. That's not just for girls- that applies to girls, boys, men, women, cats, dogs, gorillas, giraffes, no matter who or what it is, always protect yourself. By no means should you hit a girl because of an argument, disagreement, her cheating or being verbally abusive. All these things you can walk away from. But if girl is being physical, hitting, throwing objects, attempting to cut you with scissors or a knife, you defend yourself by any means necessary.

Always remember, your greatest weapon in any relationship should be your PRESENCE. When you're good to someone, the thought of you leaving will be an alarming issue. Make yourself irreplaceable. By doing so, the threat of you walking out of their life should be your weapon instead of your fist.

The best way to approach how you interact with girls is this- treat girls the exact same way you would want a man to treat your mother, grandmother, sister, female guardian or any other woman in your life that you honor and love. Treat her like the queen that she is but also know that you are a king and deserve to be treated as one also.

You will come across girls that you may feel don't deserve to be treated as queens, but a general form of respect should still be provided. Conducting yourself in these ways will make you stand out from the rest in a positive way which will increase your chances to win over the hearts of many. With these gems along with experience, the dating world will be yours for the taking.

"Now that I have her, how do I keep her?"

Soon after you get over the hump of approaching and conversing with girls you will eventually meet a special one and call her your girlfriend. Believe it or not, getting a girlfriend is not as hard as keeping her. As stated before, if you wanted and pursued her, chances are there are other guys that want and will pursue her also (even while she's in a relationship with you). So, what will make her say no to them and continue to say yes to you? Please know that you cannot control what a girl decides to do with her mind or body. All you can do is be the best option and hopefully she'll choose to be loyal to you. Here are a few things that you must know.

1. For starters, you must know how your girlfriend likes to be treated and what makes her feel loved. Find out what her Love Language is. If you're not familiar with "Love Language" google it and the both of you should take the test. By doing so, it will cut down a lot of time trying to figure out what makes your girlfriend feel loved. Often, we treat and love others the way WE like to be treated and loved. But that doesn't always work out. For example, if WE like to hug and kiss a lot (which makes US feel loved) we will do the same to our girlfriend, thinking it makes HER feel the same way it makes US feel. But that doesn't always have to be true. She may be "okay" with the hugs and kisses, but it may not make her feel loved. Her thing maybe hearing you say sweet things- complimenting her, uplifting, and speaking positively into her life. That might make her feel loved more than hugs and kisses. This is why it is so important to identify each other's love languages because if you don't, you could think you're treating and loving someone correctly but actually be missing the entire purpose unintentionally.

Father Figure

Pay attention to her. You should know her favorite color, her favorite foods, her favorite musical artists and what's guaranteed to make her smile. You obtain this information by spending not just time but QUALITY time with her. Two people can be in the same room and space but be on their phones which takes them to another room and space mentally. They're physically together but mentally far apart and separate. Phones and social media take away from personal connections. Put the phones away and the game controller down and talk. This will allow you two to bond and learn things about each other. This is considered quality time.

2. You must be able to provide for your girlfriend. "Provide what", you might ask. Provide SOMETHING-just don't come empty handed (with nothing). Figure out what she needs and provide it. There are several essential things you must provide but the most important two are security and finances. Depending on your age, finances (money) won't be a top priority (until you're older) but security will always be on the top of the list. All girls want to feel safe and protected, especially while in the presence of their boyfriend. By no means does this mean you should go around acting tough, trying to show her that you'll fight anyone to prove your love. This is actually the total opposite of making her feel safe because you're now creating unwanted tension and energy. All you need is a vibe of confidence and firmness (not cockiness) and she'll feel safe in your presence.

As you get older, finances will become more relevant. The amount of money needed will solely depend on the girl you're dealing with. Some require more. Some are okay with less. But one thing that's constant is all girls like to go out on dates every so often. They like gifts (some are okay with small gifts- some are not). They like to eat and go places to have fun and fun cost money!

Going back to the education chapter of this book, the more education you have the higher the chances of you being able to earn more money as an adult. The more money you have, the more options you have when it comes to girls. The less money you have, the less girls you will have to choose from.

As you get older, in order to have a girlfriend, you must be able to afford one. In some cases, you may meet and have a girlfriend that says money isn't an issue. She'll say that she loves you for YOU and money isn't a big deal. In rare cases this may be true but please know that generally speaking, in cases like this there's an invisible time clock winding down and sooner or later those thoughts or feelings will expire. Just think of an hourglass with small amounts of sand trickling down to the bottom. If you're struggling financially, your girlfriend will stick by your side for a moment but eventually if things don't change, you're going to possibly lose her. No one knows how long the "moment" will last- not even the girl herself, but please know that eventually that time will come.

With that being said, understand that chances are you're not going to have any REAL money until you're probably in your late twenties or early thirties. The reason why is because after high school, you will attend college or a trade school and will not be done until around 22 or 23 years old (and that's if you don't take any time off during semesters). At 23, you may pursue more education (maybe a master's degree) or land a job or start a business but all of these will be in a beginning stage so the pay could be low (starting salary) or not profiting at all if you're starting a business. The point is, it takes time to get financially going once you're done gathering the pieces to make money (education, skill set etc.) and normally the age is late 20's.

So as a teenager or young adult, your money will be limited because you don't have the resources to make real money yet.

IMPORTANT: Please do not rush to be an adult (if you don't have to). ENJOY BEING A KID with no financial responsibilities as long as possible! Small part time jobs are okay but DO NOT choose these part-time jobs over school activities, sports, music, book club's or whatever you're into. You will have the REST OF YOUR LIFE to work but you'll only get a small window of time to be kid, student and teenager so ENJOY that time and cherish it because once it's gone, you'll never be able to go back. Now there are some exceptions where some will HAVE to work because of what's going on at home and that's fine but if you don't have to, don't choose work over your childhood. If you don't get it now, you'll get it when you're much older.

Do not go out and do anything stupid to earn money that could put you in jail. One of the main reasons why young boys break the law to earn money is essentially to get girls. Having money in your pockets, dressing nice, having a car, feeling confident all leads to the ultimate goal which is getting the attention of girls. The risk you're taking (a criminal record, jail or even death) is not worth the reward. The girl you're trying to get or keep at the time, you'll vaguely remember when you get older.

Instead of chasing the money at such a young age to provide for your girlfriend, work with what you have. If she has vision, she'll be able to see the potential in you and will stick around for the final results. If she doesn't, that's fine too. Just as we talked about seasonal friends, there will also be seasonal girlfriends. It doesn't make them bad people. They may need to move out of the way to make room for the real love of your life- the person God made just for you.

3. Demand the same respect, effort, and energy that you're giving, to be received from your girlfriend in return. Treat her like the queen that she is but also expect to be

treated like the king you are as well. Relationships are not 50/ 50. They are 100/ 100. You bring your full self to the table, and she does the same.

If you're consistently focusing on meeting each other's needs, then all needs on both sides will be met but when one side takes the other for granted and stops putting in the effort, problems will occur.

Think of a relationship like car maintenance. If you just jumped in a car, drove it nonstop, didn't change the oil, ignored all of the hazard lights on the dashboard and didn't put gas in it, what do you think will happen to the car? It will break down and stop running. The same thing happens in relationships. If you don't attend to your girlfriend's needs (and vice versa) someone will shut down due to lack of attention. You must pay attention to the hazard lights in a relationship and address them to avoid future problems. You must refuel your relationship often or run the risk of the relationship running dry.

Depending on your age the car analogy might not hit home so let's think of the refrigerator in your house. Imagine if your refrigerator is filled with food and every day you went into it and took out food to eat. Eventually if you continue to just take food out without going to the grocery store to put food back in, the refrigerator will become empty. The same with relationships. If one person constantly takes from the other, without giving anything back, one will end up empty and have nothing left to give to the other. You can't just extract (take) from people without replenishing (giving back). Healthy relationships are revolving circles. That's how both party's needs are continually met.

Understand this also. We teach people how to treat us from what we allow them to say or do to us. There's an old saying that goes "Good guys always finish last" but that's not true. Good guys don't finish last. Unsure, insecure guys finish last because they allow not only girls but people in general to run over them and girls don't respect pushovers. Have conversations to set expectations and deal breakers. Again, your most valuable asset in your relationship should be your presence. Your presence is your ultimate weapon. You should never put your hands on any female unless you're forced to protect yourself. The first sign of craziness, abnormal behavior, physical violence, or extreme verbal abuse- LEAVE. These characteristics hardly ever get better with time. They only get worse so avoid the future headache by jumping ship as soon as these characteristics are detected.

Another important thing to know is if you're at the stage of your life where you're sexually active, never have unprotected sex with a girl that you're not willing to be connected with for at least the next 18 years. Having unprotected sex can or will lead to a pregnancy and once you have a child, your hopes and dreams in life will come to a screeching halt because you now have another life you're responsible for. Your time, your money, your future plans and goals will not belong to you anymore. It will belong to the child you've created. Now will you still be able to accomplish your goals after becoming a young father, sure you can but it will be EXTREMELY DIFFICULT so the best thing to do is not put yourself in that situation. God forbid you get the wrong girl pregnant and have to deal with someone who doesn't share your same morals, or view life or parenting the same as you. The wrong mother of your child will make your life miserable- emotionally and FINANCIALLY.

The perfect advice would be if you're having sex, to ALWAYS have protected sex- meaning wear a condom. But in reality, I understand that's not always the case. Usually what happens is when a young couple initially begin having sex, they'll use condoms but as time goes on, they'll stop. During this time is when pregnancies occur. My advice to you is no matter how much time passes and no matter how close and "in love" you two are, do not stop using protection.

In addition to preventing unwanted pregnancies, protected sex helps prevent sexually transmitted diseases also. There are so many sexual transmitted diseases out there such as chlamydia, gonorrhea, herpes, syphilis, HIV, AIDS- the list goes on and on. Some sexually transmitted diseases are curable, and some are not. The most common ones are extremely painful to boys such as a burning sensation while urinating and when you visit the doctor to get tested, a thin wire with a small piece of cotton (resembling a thin q tip) will get shoved down the whole on the tip of your penis (where you pee from). The pain is almost unbearable. Some have passed out/ fainted from the pain. Then they're diseases like herpes when sores and blisters cover your penis and genital area. Sounds scary? Good- that's the purpose. So be smart and always use protection.

Dealing with Heartbreak & Break ups

Unfortunately while traveling down the road of dating girls eventually you'll come across one that will hurt you/ break your heart. You're going to meet a special girl, one that checks all the boxes that you require, someone that you feel you can't live without, and she's going to leave you for someone else or just break up with you to move on. The deeper you like or love this girl, the more this will hurt.

Now if I had the remedy for this pain, I would put it in a bottle, sell it, become rich and save a lot of lives but the truth is- I do not. I can't tell you how to avoid it nor stop the hurt when it happens (and chances are, it will probably happen more than once during the course of your life). I can only give you the heads up that it probably WILL happen and provide a few tips to ease the pain some and how to get through it.

Normally heartbreaks and break ups come as a shock or surprise. Your girlfriend will have been known but to YOU, it will feel like it came out of nowhere. You can't prepare for it so when you're with your girlfriend do not subconsciously think that one day she's going to cheat or break up with you. You will ruin your relationship with those kinds of thoughts. You can't predict who this will happen with or when it will happen. But when it does happen, buckle up because it's going to be a long bumpy ride.

The severity of the initial shock of the breakup will solely depend on how it's delivered to you from your girlfriend. Her cheating or leaving you for another guy will hurt twice as much as her telling you she doesn't want to be with you anymore. Depending on your age and if you two have been intimate, that will multiply the pain times ten.

Generally after the reason for the breakup is given freely or discovered, you will probably do and say everything in your power to "fix things". Your emotions will run from hot to cold- meaning one moment you'll be mad, angry, and upset (saying "forget her") and the next you'll be sad, depressed and maybe even crying wishing she would change her mind and come back to you. All of this is standard breakup behavior. But the moment you realize that no matter what you do or say, that she's not coming back to you, that's when the REAL pain begins.

In a blink of an eye your life and daily comforts (some that you might didn't even know were comforts) will change. The phone calls, FaceTime, and text messages that you were routinely used to will now be gone. The conversations, the friendship, the dates and hanging out together will all be gone also and if you two were ever intimate, that's gone as well.

Note: Losing a girlfriend that you've been intimate with takes the hurt to a whole other level. When you get used to being intimate/ sexually involved with a girl, experiencing feelings and connections that you've never felt before, losing it can turn your world upside down. Not to mention the thought of another guy replacing you and your once girlfriend is now doing with him what she used to do with you. Thoughts and emotions like this can lead to dark mental places. Some guys have a very hard time with this and will turn to anything to ease or revenge the pain- from drinking and taking drugs to physically hurting the girl or themselves. For you, those options are NEVER the answer!

You're now forced to adapt to a new normal which is life without your now ex-girlfriend, and here's how.

Depending on how deep you were into the relationship, the breakup will cause all kinds of discomforts. You won't be able to sleep, you won't eat (lose weight), you're not going to want to hang out with friends (or be around anyone), love songs will have an entirely different meaning to you and will stir up sad feelings and emotions, and you're not going to want to talk to anyone. Many years ago, these were all just symptoms of a heart break but in today's time it's a form of depression.

The only cure to a heartbreak known to man is TIME. One might ask (especially someone in the midst of a heartbreak) "How much time"? Again, if I had that answer, I would sell it. No one can predict the amount of time needed to overcome a heartbreak. It's individually based. One might get over a heartbreak in a week or a month. Another might take a year or even years! It all depends on the person and how deep the relationship was.

In the beginning of your heartbreak it can feel like you're not going to make it. The emotional pain can feel unbearable. Your every thought will be about your now ex-girlfriend. Since there's no way to make the pain go away you must deal with it by taking it one day at a time. In some cases, one hour at a time.

Although it will be hard, try to focus and keep your mind on something, anything besides her. Stay as productively busy as possible. Idle time will be your worst enemy. If possible, find someone who you can trust and talk to them about what's going on. It's not healthy to hold these emotions in. You'll feel some comfort speaking about what you're going through. Remember- the devil wants to keep you isolated and alone so he can play with your mind and suggest ungodly actions. Although you may want to stay in your room with the lights off and lie in bed with the covers over your head, you must force yourself to get up and get into a positive environment. Also, cry if you need to. There is absolutely nothing wrong with crying. If necessary, go off to a secluded place where you have privacy, get a good cry out, get yourself together afterwards and come back refreshed. Cry, kick, talk, yell, scream, do whatever's necessary to release the pain inside of you (without causing worry or harm to others). It's not healthy to keep these feelings bottled up inside. You can physically and mentally make yourself sick by doing so. So, release those emotions as often as needed.

Heartbreaks and break ups can be very serious. Some people that aren't strong enough result to harming their ex-girlfriend or committing suicide- sometimes both. So, it's very important to know how to deal with these emotions.

Similar to all rough patches in life, think of a heartbreak as a severe thunderstorm. Sunny days are routine but every once in a while, a severe thunderstorm comes through. It's dark, intimidating, loud and scary but it normally doesn't last long. If you take shelter and wait it out, eventually the storm ends, the sun shines again, and everything goes back to normal. Your heartbreak is your severe thunderstorm. No matter how much the lightning strikes, the rain pours, and the wind blows you must find a way to survive until it ends, and the sun comes out again.

No matter how bad you feel the good news is it won't last forever. You might not know it, or it may not feel like it but you'll get better as each day passes. You just have to do things to keep your mind healthy one day at a time until you start feeling better. "Do things like what?" you might ask. Do whatever you're into to. If you're into sports, play sports. Exercise, play video games, practice on your music instrument, write songs or poems, make beats- do whatever you like to do although you may not feel up to it.

The best resource to turn to in a time like this is God. Remember, God allowed this to happen for a reason. God knows what's best for you. Deuteronomy 31:8 says "The LORD himself goes before you and will be with you; he will never leave you nor forsake you. Do not be afraid; do not be discouraged." God will not stop difficult times from occurring in your life. These times will come but God promises to be WITH YOU during the difficult times so although you may feel like you're alone, it's important for you to know that you're not. God is with you every step of the way.

Note: Sometimes God will use difficult times to get your attention. Often we tend to seek God when we're at our lowest point. This is normally when we pray more and bond with God. Remember- no one grows when they're at their highest peak (mountain top). It's hard to get through to someone who feels like they're on top of the world. People grow, develop, and learn while at their lowest peak (in the valley) because that's when they're more receptive to what's being taught. When you connect and bond with God and He delivers you from your storm, you'll know that it came from Him and only Him and it will be your duty to give Him praise and tell others what he has done for you.

With God along with releasing bottled up emotions, staying productively busy and TIME, your storm will pass (your heartbreak) and the sun in your life will shine again! Just don't give in. Almost all men have had to deal with this in some form or fashion. Weather the storm and trust the process. You'll be fine in due time. Eventually, you'll meet someone else and your ex will just be a memory.

CHAPTER 6
PEER PRESSURE

Peer pressure is the most common thing that sways boys and young men down the wrong roads of life. It's basically when you feel pressure from your bros to do, say or participate in activities that you know you shouldn't, just to "fit in". Peer pressure has a wide range- from matters that are small or light to matters that are extreme and heavy. Either way, peer pressure isn't good because no one should feel like they're being pressured to do anything, especially on the negative side.

An example of peer pressure would be this: Imagine you and your bro's hanging out somewhere and someone starts rolling up some weed, lights it and starts to smoke. All of you are standing around in a circle and the weed is being passed around from one bro to the next. Everyone hits the weed and you're the last one in the circle and now it's being passed to you. You may not smoke nor have any interest in smoking so what do you do when it's your turn to hit the weed?

Another example would be you're at school in one of your classes and there's a substitute teacher there filling in for your actual teacher. Your classmates start to get loud, playing around and disrespecting the substitute. All of your peers are playing around and having fun instead of doing their class work so what do you do? Do you join in with the fun or do you work on your class work assignment?

These are just two general examples of peer pressure situations. Any situation that you're in where most of your friends are engaging into something that you're not comfortable or have no interest in but if you say no or walk away, you won't fit in, would be a peer pressured situation. So, what do you do? What do you do when you see your bro's making fun of someone and you can see that person's feelings are being hurt but your bros continue to clown them and edge you on to join in? What do you do when everyone is drinking and pass you the bottle or stealing from a store and expect you to steal too? Your bro's pull up in a stolen car and tell you to get in- what will you do?

Generally, boys that fall victim to peer pressure are boys that aren't as confident in themselves as they should be. The number one driving factor for boys that give in to peer pressure is the want or need to fit in. The kryptonite to peer pressure is CONFIDENCE.

When you're confident and sure of yourself, you won't feel the need to fit it with others. If anything, it should be in reverse meaning your peers should feel the need to "fit in" to what you're into. Strive to be a LEADER and not a FOLLOWER. But when or if you do decide to follow someone, follow people that will lift you up instead of pull you down.

Usually the cool and popular kids in school turn out to be not so cool and popular adults. The pretty girls that everyone chases after in school turn out to be average at best as adults. If you see them years later as adults, you'll be lucky if you even recognize them. I'm saying this to say, by giving in to peer pressure, you could possibly be trying to fit in with someone or a group of people that are headed no where. I know at the current time it may seem like being with them is where you want to be but in the long scheme of things it's almost always the wrong move.

You set the example. A real "official cool kid" can tell the group with confidence "Naw, I'm good bro. I'll catch up wit y'all later" and walk away. Your leadership and confidence might just influence someone else in the group to not fall into the trap of peer pressure also. Trouble is so easy to get in to but extremely hard to get out of. Just one bad decision can possibly change the course of your life forever.

Also be mindful of the peer pressure and influence sponsored by social media and entertainment. Be careful of the pages and people you follow, the video games you play, the music you listen to, and the influencers, podcasts and shows you watch also. The content you watch works the same as the food you eat. There's an old saying that goes "you are what you eat!" Well, the same goes for the content you watch. You will be influenced, will think, and become the content that you indulge in. It will subconsciously affect your way of thinking without you even knowing it. The music you listen to will control your thoughts and emotions. The video games and movies you watch will alter your perception of reality.

Certain songs will turn you up while other songs will calm you down. We normally play the kind of music that will enhance whatever emotion we're feeling at the time. If we're trying to get mentally ready to play a sport or go to a party, we'll play something upbeat but if we're thinking about a girl or trying to chill out, we'll play something slow or mid-tempo. Also, it's not normal to see someone's head half of the way blown off or blood coming out of a body but we see it so much on video games and in movies that we don't experience a shock affect when we see real footage on our phones or on the news.

That's why it's so important to watch what you take in to your subconscious. Social media, entertainment and video games are designed to control and persuade its viewers. They want to control your mind so they can have control of YOU (for advertising, marketing purposes, financial gain and most importantly to push hidden agendas). Please know that you will become whatever you indulge in so choose wisely.

Do not allow the peer pressure of social media and entertainment to influence your thoughts and push you down roads that you know and feel in your spirit isn't for you. Proverbs 23:7 says, "For as he thinketh in his heart, so is he". Meaning you are what's in your heart. Guard your heart and protect your thoughts. Balance is important. Too much of anything isn't good for you. Every so often put your phone down for a few. Do not allow social media, entertainment, or video games to control your life. Remember your phone is supposed to be a tool- a resource, something that you use as needed. If you're not careful, you will find yourself addicted to these things.

Peer pressure is one of the hardest things to overcome as a boy/ teenager. You're literally going against what appears at the time, to be the best and most popular thing to do. Just arm yourself with two words- Confidence and Discipline. Confidence and discipline are the two major tools needed to overcome peer pressure from "friends" as well as peer pressure from "the internet". With confidence and discipline, you'll be able to decide what's cool. No one or nothing will ever have control over you!

CHAPTER 7
Dealing With the Police

Generally speaking, the purpose of the police department is to serve and protect the community. We, the people of the community are supposed to feel a sense of security when in the presence of the police- we're supposed to feel safe. Preventing crime while maintaining a sense of order was supposed to be the objective, however due to the corruption (hidden and exposed) over the last several decades, policing has been viewed drastically different. To know how to deal with ANYTHING you must first UNDERSTAND what you're dealing with. In regard to the police, let's peel back some layers to get a better understanding and then address how to deal with them.

Quick story: When I was a young boy growing up, I was never around any white people. My entire neighborhood was all black and my schoolteachers and classmates were all black. The only time I ever saw any white people on a regular basis was on TV.

Dwayne "Cooli Hi" Jones

On days when school was closed because of bad weather/ snow, I remember watching talk shows such as Donahue and Geraldo. One day there was an episode where the talk show host had an in-debt conversation with a racist group of white men called the "Skinheads". The skinheads were all white men with shaved bald heads that didn't like black people. After watching that show and a few other shows featuring the skin heads, I subconsciously formed a belief in my mind about white men with bald heads. Since I was hardly ever around any white men- especially white men with bald heads, I had no experience of my own dealing with bald headed white men. Due to the influence of what I saw on TV, I began to believe that ALL white men with bald heads were skinheads.

So as a young boy, whenever I was outside of my neighborhood in a mall or at a department store and would see a white man with a bald head, I automatically assumed that he was a skinhead. I allowed what I saw on TV to program me to subconsciously believe that all white men with bald heads were racist skinheads. A white man losing his hair because of chemotherapy or just choosing to wear a bald head as a preference never crossed my mind. A white man with a bald head meant racist skin head to me- all because of what I saw on TV. It wasn't until I got older, mature and had more personal experiences with white men that I realized that not all white men with bald heads were skinheads.

This same process applies to the police of today. Keep in mind the police are people- not robots or bots. They are people FIRST. They are people with a past, people with a view of life, people with fears, thoughts, and emotions, the same as we are. They just wear a uniform, have been granted authority and have a responsibility to conduct themselves according to the law.

Now if you take a police officer (white or black) that has little to no experience with dealing with a pro dominantly black or brown community and the only reference they have would be what they saw on the news, movies, TV shows and music videos, it's very possible that the police officers too will be influenced and will assume that black or brown people are dangerous due to what they've seen in the media. If the 5 o'clock news (local and national), social media, movies and music videos continuously show black and brown people robbing, killing and gang banging and the police officer only has this view, it's very possible that they will assume that all or the majority of the people in our community are as such.

Note: The correct thing to do would be to hire people that are well rounded and have experience in the community that they're assigned to police.

Some police officers, as well as people in general, are subconsciously programmed to believe that black people are dangerous due to the negative images that are purposely portrayed in the media.

Then there are others who don't like black or brown people for whatever reasons and decide to sign up to be a police officer in order to have legal power and authority over minorities just to mistreat them. You also have people that were bullied or mistreated when they were young and sign up to be police officers when they're older to avenge the damaged little boy that still lives and hurts inside of them and feel the need to prove something to themselves. Then you have the kind of people that are genuinely bad; they sign up to be policemen and turn into criminals with a badge. Finally, you have good law-abiding people who just have a desire to be police and genuinely respect and want to help and protect people. Take all these kinds of people, give them a uniform, gun and a badge, throw them all in one pot and you'll have a typical police department.

Now that you have a general understanding of what you could possibly be dealing with when approached, stopped or pulled over by the police, knowledge can be applied. You see, when you're stopped by a police officer, you never know which kind of the ones just mentioned you're dealing with. If you're engaging with the kind that's subconsciously influenced, you must speak and act in a certain way to combat the pre assumed false image he or she has of you. If you come across the kind that has something to prove, you don't want to say or do anything that will provoke them. If you come across the racist or the criminal there's not much you can do. Hopefully all your encounters, if any are with the good ones that want to help, serve, and protect. Also keep in mind that all these people that are police officers deal with dangerous people on a regular basis so their energy can be intense.

The goal of every interaction with the police is to do whatever is necessary to SURVIVE THE ENCOUNTER. Understand that if the world paints a picture of a criminal and the picture looks like you, then you will be pre- judged 90% of the time when encountered by the police.

Many years ago on TV shows and in movies, prisoners used to wear uniforms- all white with black stripes, resembling a zebra. We saw this all the time growing up so whenever we saw this uniform, we thought of a jailed prisoner. So, imagine during those days if we saw someone on the streets or driving in that uniform. We would prejudge and assume they're a prisoner that was released or escaped from jail. The same with the clothes you wear along with your hairstyle and the complexion of your skin. The media has painted a picture and created an image of a criminal that looks like you! So, prejudgment is headed your way whether if you like it or not.

Note: When you walk pass a lady and she clutch her purse tightly assuming you might attempt to snatch her purse, chances are she's never experienced being robbed. She's reacting from how she's been programmed to act by what she's viewed on the news and media.

The million dollar question is, "Who's behind painting this criminal picture of you and why is it being portrayed all over the world?"

Knowing about the agenda of making people believe you're a criminal along with the types of police officers you may encounter should give you a heads up on how to act when confronted by the police. Again- just SURVIVE THE ENCOUNTER.

Do not make sudden or aggressive moves. If pulled over, keep your hands visible at all times. Do not reach for ANYTHING, especially things in your pockets. Ask the officer to get your wallet for you. Say yes sir or mam- No sir or mam. Be polite and as non-threatening as possible no matter what the police say or how they treat you. If you're being physically assaulted protect yourself as much as possible by guarding your head and face but do not fight back. It will only give them more of a reason to hurt you.

Just SURVIVE THE ENCOUNTER. You can always circle back, file a complaint and press charges AFTER the encounter is over and you're safe from harm. Do and say whatever you must (as non- confrontational as possible) to get you through the encounter. You shouldn't have to stoop to these measures just to survive but unfortunately this is the world and reality we live in. It's not right. It's unjust and not fair but that's not important. The most important thing is for you to understand what's out there regarding police and how to survive a dangerous encounter- if necessary. That's all that matters.

CHAPTER 8
Coping with Life's Ups & Downs

When going through this thing we call life, there's one thing you can always count on and that is you will come across hard and difficult times. No man or woman on this planet is exempt from the ups and downs of life. Good times are the majority, but bad times will come. There's no way to avoid it.

As stated previously, life is like the weather. Most days the sun will be out but occasionally it will rain and every so often a severe thunderstorm will happen. Then after the storm, the sun comes out again. In the words of the R&B group New Edition, "Sunny days, everybody loves them, but can you stand the rain?" The sunny days are when everything in your life is moving along smoothly- things are okay. The rainy days are when you're having a bad day. Severe thunderstorms are times when your life feels like it's been turned upside down.

Since there's nothing you can do to avoid hard times you must know what can be done to get through them. You must know how to survive during a storm in your life until it passes, and the sun shines again. Actually, hard times (storms) are needed because it makes you appreciate the good times (the sunshine) but more importantly, it brings you closer to God (well it should because depending on how severe the storm is, the only way to get through it will be to turn to God). Let's discuss some of the most common rough patches of life and how to deal with them. First up- betrayals and disappointments.

Betrayal & Disappointments

No one in this world is perfect. Everyone is flawed. There was only one man that walked the face of this earth that was perfect, and His name was Jesus. None of us are Him so since no one is perfect, we can't expect perfection from anyone.

People will let you down. Not some but all people have the capability of letting you down. Your mom, dad, brother, sister, best friend all could possibly one day disappoint you in some way. The higher the expectations you have for someone, the greater the chance of that person disappointing you. What you feel when a classmate lets you down can't compare to what you feel when Mom or Dad lets you down because your expectations are higher for Mom and Dad.

Not only people, but situations will disappoint also. You might try out for an activity or sport, invest your all into it and not make the team. You might be looking forward to an event or a trip and at the last minute, you're told it's cancelled, or you specifically can't go. It might be a job, a school, or a program that you really want to be a part of- you apply, give it your all and not get accepted. Things like these will happen all the time during the course of your life.

Rejection is painful. It makes you feel unwanted. In some cases, it makes you feel alienated- like you're all alone. But here's the underlying beauty in rejection that I want you to know. When you're connected to God and being the best version of yourself by putting in the time and effort to achieve a goal, the rejection is actually a blessing! Remember, God always knows what's best for you. He sees your beginning, middle and end. That team, job, or school that you desire to be a part of so much, might not be the best fit for you in the long run. God might have something in mind that's 10x better! When you're connected to God, rejections are blessings. Although it hurts, it's stopping you from going one way, to set you up to go in the right direction- which is Gods way.

Since you know that in life, occasionally people and situations will disappoint you, it's important to know how to deal with it. Again, with situational disappointments, your approach should be "this isn't for me. God has something better". It's a blessing (and this even applies to some people also)! The key is to stay connected with God so He can direct your path. But when it comes to people, it's a different approach.

Everyone has flaws (including yourself). Knowing this confirms that disappointments can come from anyone you know so it's safe to assume that people will disappoint. One day you will confide in someone by telling them a secret, make them swear not to tell ANYONE and that person is going to tell someone.

Note: If you don't want something repeated, I advise not to tell anyone at all.

It happens all the time. Now I don't suggest anticipating, provoking, or expecting disappointments from people but I do suggest for you to be mentally ready when or if a disappoint occurs.

The most painful part of being disappointed by someone is the actual shock. You might say to yourself "I can't believe John would do this!" Well, John isn't perfect so believe it. Give a little wiggle room or cushion for disappointments. Also lower your expectations of people when you notice character flaws. In most cases when disappointments happen, there were signs leading up to it. There's only one that will never disappoint you and that is God. Understanding this will allow you to set reasonable expectations when dealing with people so when disappointments occur, the sting isn't so bad.

Betrayal

Betrayal on the other hand hurts in a different way. A person can disappoint you inadvertently or unintentionally, but betrayal is a personal attack therefore the hurt is intensified. During the course of your life, some of the closest people you know might betray you. A girlfriend might cheat on you. One of your best friends might attempt to date your current girlfriend or your ex-girlfriend. A close friend or even a family member might steal from you or arrange for something bad to happen to you. Betrayal is personal. A stranger or someone you hardly know could never betray you because betrayal comes from within your inner circle, not outsiders.

Loyalty is a popular word that everyone uses these days but only a few people practice it. Under certain circumstances best friends, girlfriends and family members could possibly betray you. They'll smile in your face and then drag your name through the mud behind your back.

Usually the root of betrayal is either greed, jealousy, or envy (in some cases, all). People wanting what you have, and it isn't always material things. In most cases it's not material. People who betray you usually want your internal light. They admire your presence, your aura- the attention you receive when you walk in a room, your personality, your charm- they admire the light that's inside of you that shines everywhere you go. They want it but can't have it so that's where the jealousy and envy stems from.

Unlike disappointment's betrayals are hardly ever forecasted. It comes from the closest people to you, so you hardly ever see it coming and it usually hurts you to the core. Like all emotional pains, if you're not strong enough, these painful situations can cause you to think about hurting yourself and THAT CAN NEVER HAPPEN!

When or if you're ever betrayed, forgive the person but don't EVER forget. The forgiveness is for YOU, not for them. If you don't forgive them, you'll carry around that pain and possibly take it out on others in your life that had nothing to do with it. Forgiving them allows you to release the hurt and not carry it around with you. Regarding the person who betrayed you, it's up to you whether if you should keep them in your life. Once trust is broken it's almost impossible to gain back but the key word is "almost". It's a judgement call regarding cutting the person off or keeping them around. There's no right or wrong answer but if you do decide to give the betrayer a second chance, don't ever forget what this person is capable of and do not put yourself in a position to be betrayed by them again.

Betrayals and disappointments are common life experiences. Practically all people have experienced them both and if you haven't by the time you're reading this, sooner or later you will. You can't control what happens. You can only control how you respond to it. Just always keep in mind that people will let you down, sometimes on purpose, sometimes unintentionally. Things will not go your way. People that are close to you will hurt you. This is all because we as people are flawed so disappointment and betrayals are an unfortunate part of life that we all must deal with. There's only ONE person we all can rely and depend on. ONE that will never disappoint or let us down and that ONE person is God. So, brace yourself for betrayals and disappointments. They have come, are coming, or maybe coming again. Anchor yourself in God so when the strong stormy winds blow, the bad weather won't whisk you away. Stay solid, ten toes down until the storm ends. Deuteronomy 31-8 says "The Lord himself goes before you and will be with you; he will never leave you nor forsake you. Do not be afraid; do not be discouraged."

Endure the pain (storm), bond with God and before you know it, it will be over, and the sun will be shining again.

Death

Another rough patch of life that's extremely difficult to deal with is death- losing someone you love. The death of a loved one- the forbidden topic. Hardly no one wants to talk or even think about it. But unfortunately, it's something that we all will have to deal with.

Death is the inevitable. Everything that lives will one day die (well fleshly die). For all that believe in Christ know heaven awaits when we leave this earth. In the Bible, John 14: 1-4 Jesus said "Let not your heart be troubled; you believe in God, believe also in Me. In My Father's house are many mansions; if it were not so, I would have told you. I go to prepare a place for you. And if I go and prepare a place for you, I will come again and receive you to Myself; that where I am, there you may be also. And where I go you know, and the way you know." When Thomas (one of Jesus disciples) said "Lord, we don't know where you are going, so how can we know the way?" Jesus answered, "I am the way and the truth and the life. No one comes to the Father except through me." John 14: 6.

No one can be loss when you know where they are. The Bible also says in 2 Corinthians 5:8 "We are confident, yes, well pleased rather to be absent from the body and to be present with the Lord." Meaning when someone dies believing in Christ, their bodies sleep in the grave, but their soul immediately returns to Christ until Christ comes back and that's when the soul is joined with their new glorified body.

Knowing all of this is comforting but it doesn't entirely take away the pain you feel when a loved one dies. You will still miss them and wish they were still here. This process is called grieving. There's no right or wrong way to grieve nor is there a time limit on grieving. Just know that you can always keep them alive in your heart by sharing and cherishing the memories of that loved one, viewing pictures and videos and talking about them to others. If your loved one was sick, rest assure that they are no longer suffering in pain, they are now free from the pressures of this cruel world that we live in. If it was an unexpected death, create something in honor of their name (a charity or event) to continue their legacy. Again, there's no right or wrong way to get through. Do whatever it takes to soothe your wounded heart.

When you lose a loved one (especially someone extremely close like a parent, sibling, or best friend) you'll never get over it, but with God you will get through it. Your life might not ever be the same, but you must find a way to push through and keep living. The loved one that passed away would not want you to be down in the dumps dragging through life. They would want you to continue living life to the fullest!

Side Note: Regarding attending funerals, please know that funerals are for the LIVING not the dead. The person that passed away is no longer inside of that body. They are with God. When you or someone attends a funeral, the main purpose should be to show love and support to the family and friends- the ones that are still alive, grieving and are in need. Paying respect to the dead is fine but the most important part is supporting the grieving family members.

Death is a part of life. The longer you live, unfortunately the more deaths you will experience. Some will be expected (someone being sick in the hospital and slowly passes away) and some unexpected- the shockers (the here today- gone tomorrow's, car accidents, murders, heart attacks etc.). The unexpected shockers are the most difficult because there's no time to prepare and brace yourself unlike someone being up in age, sick and confined to a hospital bed.

Find comfort in knowing that God will never bring anything to your doorstep that you can't handle. He won't stop what's coming your way, but He promises to be by your side the ENTIRE WAY. It might not feel like it at times but He's ALWAYS there with you and rest assure that one day, you'll see your loved ones again on the other side in Glory!

Mental Heath

Dealing with the many varieties of rough patches of life from betrayals and disappointments to the passing of a loved one, and everything in between can weigh heavy on the mind. Difficult times can take you to dark places which can lead to depression or other forms of mental illness. Having a safe place- a listening ear (that won't pass judgement), or a shoulder to cry on is the best way to avoid falling into dark places and that usually means talking to a therapist.

Since we go to the doctors when we are physically hurt or sick and for general checkups, the dentist to take care of our teeth, and the eye doctor for vision and glasses, it only makes sense to see a therapist to maintain a healthy state of mind. Depending on your age, you may not be able to see a therapist on your own, but you can let your mom or dad know that you would like to talk to one. If a therapist isn't an option, try speaking to a school counselor, a teacher you trust, a mentor or anyone that you feel comfortable speaking to. Your mind requires just as much medical attention as your body, probably even more because your mind dictates how your body functions. Don't ever hesitate to reach out to someone when you're feeling sad or depressed. If not addressed, these feelings can cause major emotional problems and like all sicknesses, the longer you wait, the worse it gets.

Also it's important to know that it's okay to cry. For years there has been a false narrative implying that boys/ men are not supposed to cry. Mental/ emotional pain is TOTALLY different from physical pain. When you're going through a mental crisis it's best to release those emotions instead of keeping them bottled up within. As stated before, if you need to, find a secluded place where you can be alone and let a good cry out. Crying may not resolve your issues, but it will definitely give you a sense of release which will provide you with a clearer head to address what's going on.

Feeling sad or depressed about how things are going in your life will happen at times. There's nothing abnormal about these feelings. We all get sad at times. Every so often you will receive some bad news, or your life might not be going the way you thought it would go. Things are not going to go as planned and people and situations will let you down but if you find yourself in the dumps longer than you should be, talk to someone about it and seek help.

Isolating yourself from others, sleeping all day, lying in bed with the covers over your head, staying in dark rooms and not eating are all signs of depression. No matter how hard it may seem, you must fight to get out of those dark spaces. Force yourself to get out of bed and get dressed. Open the shades and allow the sunlight to shine in. The devil dwells in darkness. God is light! Allow God to enter your room. Keep your room and your surroundings clean and neat. Again, the devil dwells in confusion, mess, and clutter. God on the other hand lives in clarity, neatness, and cleanliness.

A healthy mind increases the chance of a healthy body and a better quality of life. So, take care of your mind the same as you would take care of your body and never hesitate to ask for help when needed.

Life is full of ups and downs. Peaks and valleys. As stated before, the peaks are the good times, times we all love but the valleys, which are the hard times are the most challenging. Always keep in mind that the valleys are the most difficult times but it's also the time when we grow and learn valuable life lessons and receive wisdom. When we're at the peak, it's hard for God to get our attention because everything is good so sometimes a storm is needed just to get our attention. We hear Gods voice clearly when in the valley because we're in need of His help. The valley is where He shapes and molds us so when He brings us out of the valley and back to the mountain top (the peak), it's important to remember the lessons that were taught in the valley.

Pain also gives birth to the most beautiful creations. Your favorite love song or movie was probably written and inspired by someone who experienced a heart break. So, take the good along with the bad and no matter what, keep pushing forward.

CHAPTER 9
The Power of Prayer

Prayer- the sacred and spiritual key that unlocks the doors of heaven and gives us direct access to God. Without God it is impossible to get through the obstacles of life. During the course of your life, it's guaranteed that you'll run into situations that no human being on earth will be able to help you get through. God and only God will be your resource- your problem solver so it's important for you to know that you must pray and stay connected to Him. Psalm 37: 25 says "I have been young, and now am old; Yet I have not seen the righteous forsaken, Nor his descendants begging bread." No one that walks with God will go without their needs. Not your wants but your needs.

Prayer changes things. It opens locked doors and moves the unmovable. When life hits you with a hard right hook you must know where to turn to recover and get back on your feet. When you're pursuing your life goals and dreams and in need of Gods favor, prayer is how you get it. When you or someone you love are sick and in need of healing or when you're in trouble with the law (whether it's your fault or you being at the wrong place at the wrong time) and in need of a breakthrough, prayer is the answer. Miracles are REAL and attainable, but you must tap into the source from which miracles come from and that source is our living God.

Prayer is an intimate and personal conversation that you have with God. There's no right or wrong way to pray. God is your father but He's also your friend. Speak to Him with a genuine and open heart and He will hear your prayers.

Not only should you pray when in need of a miracle, you should also pray and thank God for what you already have. Before you ask God for ANYTHING, always thank Him for EVERYTHING. Giving God praise for the countless blessings that are currently in your life, opens the portal for more blessings to come. Don't forget to pray for others as well, the same as you would like others to pray for you.

After you pray, you must BELIEVE that God will answer your prayers. You must have faith. Faith is the confidence or trust in God and His promises, and the assurance of things that are hoped for and not seen. In today's world seeing is believing. People generally need to see things to believe but faith doesn't work that way. With faith, you must believe something will happen when there's no path, vision, or a clue of how it will happen. Believing without seeing. Faith activates Gods favor because it shows that you trust Him. In the Bible, 2 Corinthians 5: 7 says "For we walk by faith, not by sight." God is faithful so believe that he will answer your prayers.

You are human so it's natural to have some doubts but keep in mind what Jesus said in Matthew 17: 20-21 "Because of your unbelief; for assuredly, I say to you, if you have faith as a mustard seed, you will say to this mountain, 'Move from here to there,' and it will move; and nothing will be impossible for you." Faith as small as the size of a mustard seed can do the impossible but when praying, be mindful that what you're asking for must be within His will. Sometimes we pray for things and situations that are against His will (not knowing of course) and then wonder why our prayers aren't being answered. It must be within Gods will.

When doing this thing called life, you can't do it alone. You will need Gods guidance. All blessings come from God- the good and the "bad". When you're connected to God even the devil himself must get permission from God to approach you. The key word is approach. There's a cliche saying you've probably heard before that goes "the devil made me do it." That's not possible. The devil has no authority over you so he can't make you do ANYTHING! He can only approach and present things to you and hope that you will choose what he's offering. But even when you do occasionally choose the wrong path, God will use what was intended for bad and turn it around and make it good. One of the major benefits of acquiring God's grace and mercy.

People are only vessels. Meaning God uses people to deliver his blessings to you. Don't let anyone trick you into believing that they are your source for fortune, health, happiness, or opportunity. They are just the middleman. All things come from God so always give God praises- not man.

Keep a consistent and meaningful prayer coming out of your heart daily. Pray for God to give you wisdom so you can navigate through life and make the best choices. It's a cold and evil world out there. There's no need to face it alone when you don't have to. One of my favorite quotes from the Bible is this- Proverbs 3:5- 6 "Trust in the Lord with all your heart, And lean not on your own understanding; In all your ways acknowledge Him, And He shall direct your paths." Stay connected through prayer and allow God to direct your path.

CHAPTER 10
The Transition from Boys to Men

The transition from childhood to adulthood is simple. Contrary to state laws it has nothing to do with your age. Turning 18 nor 21 years old doesn't automatically make you an adult. It only makes you a "legal adult" meaning you can now be held accountable from a legal perspective. Becoming an adult simply means being responsible for your own actions and being able to fully take care of yourself financially, physically, and mentally without any assistance from others (others meaning the people or person who raised you). That's it. You're not "grown" just because you're a certain age. You're "grown" when you're able to live and survive on your own.

Since this is true, that means there are some 19- and 20-year-old adults out there but there are also some 30- and 40-year-old children out there as well (legally they're adults but mentally they are still children). Until you're able to put a roof over your head, feed and clothe yourself, commute from one place to another, be responsible enough to be places where you should be and on time (ex. class or work) and live a productive life without needing assistance from others, you're not an adult (only exceptions would be people that are experiencing mental and/ or heath challenges). It's doesn't matter how old you are if you still must depend on Mom, Dad, or a guardian to take care of you. The same applies with boys turning into men but the only difference is, the world gets a little colder.

Life is not fair. Everyone isn't promised a seat at the table. No one gives a man anything. Everything a man gets, he must compete and work hard for. Compassion is usually shown to women and children, not men so bundle up. It's cold out there. Women and children typically rely on men to provide and protect but men must rely on themselves while turning to God for assistance. As I mentioned earlier, enjoy being a child, teenager, or young adult as long as you can because once you convert over to manhood, there's no turning back.

When you're able to answer the adult question just mentioned with a "yes" you've officially become a man. But don't settle with being just a man. Strive to become a good man, a great man, a God-fearing man, a man of good integrity and honor. To do so, indulge in these practices.

Never make decisions while in an emotional state-angry or happy. It's always logic over emotions. Making decisions based off emotions/ how you feel (at the time) normally leads to disasters.

Practice and show empathy to others. Put yourself in other people's shoes to see their point of view when necessary. Doing so will open an entirely different perspective when attempting to resolve conflicts with others.

Value people's time by always being on time. Things happen and if so, reach out and tell people if you can't make it or if you're running late. Remember, if you stay ready, you'll never have to get ready!

Your word is your bond. If you say you're going to do something or be somewhere, do it or be there. Always say what you mean and mean what you say. Honor your promises because if broken without a good reason, your integrity can be damaged beyond repair.

I'll stop here and pass the baton to the greatest teacher on earth to guide you the rest of the way- EXPERIENCE. I hope that you fulfill Gods purpose for your life, and I wish you all the best! Always remember, no matter who says they love you, God loves you more. Stay connected to Him and enjoy your journey!

God Bless.

About the Author

Dwayne "Cooli Hi" Jones originally started his musical career as a hip hop recording artist. What distinguished this Baltimore native from other artists in that genre is the compelling subject matter, smooth delivery, and unique lyrical content. With his baritone laden rhymes, he gives his fans an incredible visual experience as he narrates stories of common urban tales and life experiences. Overall, it's his dynamic ability to add a touch of pure human emotions that turns even the toughest hip hop skeptic into a fan. So it's no surprise that songwriting was this talented artist's next exploration.

In 2001 Cooli Hi was featured on Sisqo's Hit Single "Can I Live" Produced by Teddy Riley. Since his debut on the single from the multi-platinum album, Return of the Dragon, Cooli Hi has performed with such notable groups as Dru Hill and The Backstreet Boys.

Dwayne "Cooli Hi" Jones

This experience gave him the opportunity to perform on MTV's Total Request Live (TRL), CBS This Morning and the historic 1st Annual BET Music Awards. In addition to countless performances in the United States, Cooli Hi has entertained audiences all over the world; from

Africa to Scotland to London - including a performance on Top Of The Pops, a syndicated show in London that features the biggest acts in Hip Hop, Rock and Pop music.

In 2006 a childhood friend introduced him to a BMI executive with the intentions of showcasing his hip hop writing talents. As the BMI executive listened, he periodically stopped the music, curious to find out who wrote the chorus's on the tracks. When he discovered that Cooli Hi wrote and arranged all of the choruses, he asked a question that unleashed one of Cooli's many hidden talents. "Have you ever considered writing an entire R&B song?" That simple inquiry undoubtedly unlocked the initiative for this exceptional musician to transition from writing hooks, to writing breathtaking songs that cover an array of music genres. As with hip hop, his lyrics still target the pulse of everyday life and the foundation for every song starts with the consciousness and passion of pure human sentiment. As you listen to songs written by Cooli Hi, your emotions will connect as the phrases turn, and the melodies soar! That is his formula for timeless music!

Father Figure

Realizing his strengths in Songwriting, and combining that with a style influenced by great artists of the past Dwayne "Cooli Hi" Jones continues to touch the hearts and souls of many with his gift and never follows a trend. His past experiences have molded an artist who realizes that music is not an avenue to wealth, but an outlet of expression that holds the power to touch lives and lift spirits. More importantly, for him, music is a way of life!